Portrait of the compiler of the Imitation

(See Introduction, p. xiii)

Perfection = Complete Devoutness.

yas
if a

THE IMITATION OF CHRIST

PREFACE

IN preparing the present translation of the *Imitation* the editor has made use of several English translations. At the same time, however, he has everywhere consulted the autograph copy of Thomas à Kempis, completed in the year 1441. The division into verses is based on the system of A Kempis, while the second and third books follow both A Kempis and the German translation by Paul Hagen. Dr. Hagen has authorized the translation of these two books for the present edition, and where the version of A Kempis differs from that of the manuscripts used by Hagen, the latter has usually been followed.

INTRODUCTION

AMONG all the books ever written in Europe and America, none have enjoyed such a wide circulation as the *De Imitatione Christi,* or *Imitation of Christ.* According to the catalogue of the British Museum, the *Imitation* has been for four hundred years next to the Bible the most widely read book in the world. "After the Gospel," writes one prominent Catholic scholar in America, "the *Imitation* undoubtedly is the book that reflects with the greatest perfection the light which Jesus Christ brought us down from heaven. . . . Nowhere else do we find the same doctrine inculcated with a more persuasive eloquence than in the unpretending little volume that all of us have a hundred times perused." [1]

John Wesley wrote in the preface of the edition he edited himself: "Such is the strength, spirit, and weight of every sentence that it is scarce possible, without injury to the sense, to add or diminish anything. . . . A serious mind will never be sated with it, though it were read a thousand times over; for those general principles are the seeds of meditation, and the stores they contain are never exhausted. And herein it greatly resembles the Holy Scriptures, that under the plainest words, there is

---

1—A. J. Thebaud, "Who Wrote the Imitation of Christ?" in *American Catholic Quarterly Review,* 1883, p. 650.

divine hidden virtue, continually flowing into the soul of a pious and attentive reader, and by the blessing of God transforming it into His image."

Milman, in his *History of Latin Christianity*,[2] testifies that "in one remarkable book was gathered and concentrated all that was elevating, passionate, profoundly pious, in all the older mystics. Gerson, Ruysbroeck, Tauler, all who addressed the heart in later times, were summed up, and brought into one circle of light and heat, in the one single volume, the *Imitation of Christ*. That this book supplies some imperious want in the Christianity of mankind, that it supplied it with a fullness and felicity which left nothing, at this period of Christianity, to be desired, its boundless popularity is the one unanswerable testimony. . . . The book absolutely and entirely supersedes and supplies the place of the spiritual teacher, the spiritual guide, the spiritual comforter; it is in itself that teacher, guide, comforter. According to its notion of Christian perfection, Christian perfection is attainable by its study and by the performance of its precepts; the soul needs no other mediator, at least no earthly mediator, for its union with the Lord."

It would require several large volumes to reproduce all the eulogies that have flowed from the pens of those millions of men and women who have read with profound admiration the *Imitation of Christ*. Together with the Bible it has found its way into the remotest regions, eagerly devoured by Christian and pagan, by civilized and barbarian. Who knows how many stubborn hearts it has softened, how

2—Vol. IX, pp. 161-163.

many aches it has healed, how much hatred it has melted as the sun melts the snow in spring?

However, in analyzing the teachings of the *Imitation,* one is immediately made aware of the fact that this book was writen in the Middle Ages. It was addressed to various classes of people in a time when few men questioned the doctrine of eternal damnation and when the terms evolution, theosophy, modernists, and atheists were seldom employed. Many editions of the *Imitation* have appeared in which a number of passages were eliminated, although nothing was said about such omissions by the editors. Protestant admirers have imagined that the work was a precursor of the Reformation, and that a few omissions would make it seem a Protestant book. But the plain truth remains that it was composed when Western Europe, the cradle of modern civilization, was still dominated by the doctrines of the Roman Catholic Church.

Nevertheless no apology is needed for the authors of the *Imitation,* for the enlightened student of history does not expect to find modern conditions in medieval countries and times. He would not try to make the Bible appear as a text-book on science, any more than he would try to harmonize the contents of the *Imitation* with the teachings of the religious cults which have come into existence since the opening of the nineteenth century.

At present nobody knows exactly how the *Imitation* was composed. The authorities do agree that the book was written during the first quarter of the fifteenth century in that part of the Low Countries which is now included in the kingdom of Holland. That Thomas à Kempis composed a part of it is also generally admitted. But how large a part was his, and who the other authors were, is not known to anybody. That it will ever be known is highly improbable, unless science should open up new means of searching into the lives of men and women who left no visible records of their activities.

The *Imitation* may be called the Gospel of the Devotio Moderna, that great religious and educational revival which originated in the Low Countries and spread far beyond the boundaries of its native soil. It contains the teachings of a certain Gerard Groote, who founded two institutions, called Brethren and Sisters of the Common Life, and Congregation of Windesheim. The influence exerted by these two institutions was altogether out of proportion to the attention they have thus far received from Dutch historians. Their history has been neglected in the past, partly because the men and women connected with them lived peaceful lives, never sought notoriety, never preached open heresy nor rebellion, nor did they ever cause disturbances of any kind. If only they had interfered in political affairs, as did Savonarola, or had attacked the church as an institution, as did Wycliffe and Luther; if only one of them had been publicly condemned by a great council, as was Huss, or had founded a great church, as did Calvin, their institutions would have become much more widely known.

Instead of that they merely taught and preached love, obedience, peace, and humility, fed the poor, sheltered the homeless, cured the sick, reformed monasteries, corrected abuses, and wrote books like the *Imitation*. They shared the fate of the "hidden saints," whose names seldom if ever appear in our newspapers, but whose influence is often much greater than that of a heretic, or a hero, or a scoundrel. Even Jesus of Nazareth, who was perhaps the greatest of all teachers, created comparatively little stir in his day. Few text-books on Roman history mention his name. Had he but gone to Rome at the head of a Jewish army, had he but seized the city and held it for a short time, the story of his life would have been told in all the text-books. Instead of that he died on the cross, forsaken by almost all his followers, so that his death caused not a ripple upon the sea of the old history. Nevertheless he conquered Rome more effectively than any other man ever did, and in a certain sense he rules there still.

It was the same way with some of the Brethren of the Common Life. Two or three of them wrote the greatest book of the time, the *Imitation of Christ*. Erasmus, the intellectual king of Europe and prince of the humanists, was educated in two of their schools and dormitories for a period of twelve years. Alexander Hegius, the greatest educator in Europe at the end of the fifteenth century, taught the principles of the Devotio Moderna in Deventer, which was the center of the movement, and where Erasmus had spent eight or nine years as a boy. His school counted twenty-two hundred pupils, while Eton, much more famous in history, had at the most one hundred and fifty, and the best known school in Italy, a paltry seventy.

Several hundred schools were founded or reformed by members and pupils of the brotherhood. Luther attended their school at Magdeburg for a year, while Calvin spent four years in the dormitory of

Montaigu in Paris, founded by Standonck, a pupil of the brethren. Another pupil was Cardinal Cusa, the famous mathematician and philosopher. Wimpheling, Bucer, Beatus Rhenanus, Agricola, Gansfort, Pope Adrian VI, who at one time was the tutor of Charles V, Dringenberg, who made the school of Schlettstadt more famous than that of Strasbourg, Murmellius, the great pedagogue of Münster —these and thousands of other prominent men were or had been connected with the brotherhood. What the brethren themselves accomplished in the realms of education and religion, and how they affected modern civilization, cannot be stated precisely. Although the present writer has devoted a book of considerable size to the history of the movement as a whole,[3] he has merely hinted at the possible influence the brethren may have had.

It is sufficient for us to know at the present that the *Imitation* was produced by followers of Gerard Groote. The teachings found in every part of this book are his teachings, and its influence is the outcome of his work. If one hundred or two hundred years ago a history of the Devotio Moderna had appeared, very few books would have been devoted to the authorship of the *Imitation*. Now there are so many that no human being will ever be able to read them all. But not all of these works have been written in vain. Thanks to the activities of their authors, we are now in a position to solve many difficult problems.

The compiler of the *Imitation of Christ* was Thomas à Kempis, or, rather, Thomas Hemerken

3—*The Christian Renaissance: A History of the Devotio Moderna,* New York (The Century Co.), 1925.

of Kempen. He was born in the town of Kempen
in the diocese of Cologne. The date of his birth
is not certain. Some writers claim it must be placed
in the year 1379 or 1380; others, in the year 1380
or 1381. His father was called John Hemerken,
or John with the little hammer, for he earned his
living with his hammer, though he also owned a
tract of land. That both Thomas and his brother
John à Kempis were not mere phantoms invented
by chronicle writers, is shown by a document written at Kempen in the year 1402, in which the sale
of their father's home is attested.

Thomas à Kempis spent seventy-two years in the
monastery of Mount St. Agnes, near Zwolle. He
was highly venerated for his piety, and the people of
Zwolle for many generations took great pride in
claiming him as one of their own. It was said that
several portraits had been painted of him during
his lifetime. According to the most reliable authorities in Holland, the portrait reproduced on the
frontispiece of the present edition of the *Imitation* is
that of Thomas à Kempis.

In 1392 the fame of Deventer's cathedral school
had reached the duchy of Guelders, in which
Kempen was situated. Whether it was due to the
presence of the Brethren of the Common Life or to
the reforms initiated on Groote's advice, certain
it is that many parents were anxious to have their
boys educated at Deventer. In Thomas's case there
was an additional reason for his going there. His
brother John had been a Brother of the Common
Life, and was now living at Windesheim. In 1392
Thomas arrived at Deventer. "When I came to
study at Deventer," he wrote afterward, "I went to

Windesheim, where my brother was living. He told me to visit Florentius Radewijns." Eager to follow John's advice, for John knew the vicar well, Thomas came to Radewijns, the leader of the brethren in Deventer. He was not a wealthy boy; he could not even pay for his board and lodging. Radewijns took compassion on him and invited him to stay at his house. Thus fortune smiled upon him from the first day.

Not only did Radewijns provide him with lodging, but he gave him books and paid his tuition at the school. His teacher at that time was a certain John Boheme. One day Thomas brought him the tuition fee. "Who gave it to you?" the teacher asked. "Radewijns," was the boy's reply. "Then take it back to your kind master," said the teacher. It takes very little imagination to see how much the friendship of a man like Radewijns meant to the boys then attending the cathedral school. Thomas must have told his parents about it, and the other boys. His parents in turn probably mentioned his experiences to other parents. In this way even before the close of the fourteenth century the influence of Gerard Groote was being felt in homes far beyond the Yssel valley, where Deventer was situated.

But the brethren-house at Deventer was too small to lodge school-boys. Radewijns, therefore, looked around for some other quarters, and sent Thomas to a certain devout woman, doubtless one of Groote's disciples. How long the boy stayed with her we do not know. It seems that after a few years he lived with the brethren again, for he tells of experiences in the brethren-house: "All I earned," he writes, "I gave to the community; the rest I needed was

given by Florentius. Here I learned to read and
write the Holy Scriptures and books on moral subjects, but it was chiefly through the sweet conversation of the Brethren that I was inspired
yet more strongly to despise the world. I took
pleasure in their godly conduct. Never before could
I recollect to have seen such men, so devout and
fervent."

What Florentius Radewijns did reminds us of
Groote's work among the school-boys at Deventer.
He also had often invited them to come to his house,
and had given them work to do. Some of these
boys became Brethren of the Common Life, though
at the time they visited Groote they were living still
in private homes. Thomas à Kempis too was first
lodged with a pious woman, as soon as Radewijns
found a place for him. Later he was asked to become a real inmate of the brethren-house. Perhaps
Thomas lived only one year with the brethren at
Deventer, as his own remarks seem to prove, but
the influence of Radewijns had been shaping his
young mind before he reëntered the brethren-house.
Later he wrote: "During seven years of my life
[1392-99] I experienced the wonderful compassions
of Florentius Radewijns." Add to this that his own
brother John had lived with Radewijns in the first
brethren-house at Deventer, and the conclusion is
justified that when Thomas began to preach and
write, he repeated the maxims of Groote and
Radewijns, the two founders of the new brotherhood, the two men who inaugurated the Devotio
Moderna.

Thomas à Kempis never could have chosen a
better time to "learn to read and write the sacred

writings" than in the year 1398-99. It was in the summer of 1398 that the two institutions of Gerard Groote at Deventer passed through the greatest crisis that ever was to threaten their existence. In the brethren-house at Deventer the men had lived a semi-monastic life, undisturbed by quarrels, feuds, and hostile attacks. Then came the terrible pestilence in June, taking the lives of nearly all the experienced members. First in the vicarage of Radewijns, and later in the "House of Florentius," or the real brethren-house, they had for more than fourteen years tried to do what they believed Christ had commanded in the Beatitudes. They had conscientiously endeavored to "despise the world," to "remain unknown," to "offer themselves to God," and to "subdue the flesh."

Let us in imagination visit Deventer. It is early in the month of June that the pestilence has made its appearance in the brethren-house. More than half of the inmates have the disease, while most of the others have hurriedly fled, taking many school-boys with them. Thomas à Kempis remains at Deventer, where for six years he has followed in the footsteps of his beloved Radewijns. The pious cook in the brethren-house and all the older members have died. In the brethren-house Thomas has found the spiritual exercises of John Ketel, the cook, and of Lubbert ten Bossche, besides those of the other dead brothers. Thomas finds himself practically the sole possessor of the jealously guarded treasures in the library. Most precious to him seem the "devout exercises" of Groote and Radewijns, of which a few excerpts are given below:

Likewise after the example of Bernard, utter no word by which thou mayest seem to be very religious, or endowed with knowledge. Resolve to avoid and abhor all public disputations which are but wranglings for success in argument, or the appearance thereof (such as the disputations of graduates in theology at Paris), and take no part therein. . . . So also I will never argue with any one in private unless it is certain that some good end shall follow. . . . My first resolution is to desire no further preferment. . . . According to the rule of the primitive church thou canst not hold several benefices. . . . Let there be a daily fast which doth consist in not wholly satisfying the appetite. . . . All philosophers advise this, specially Seneca and Aristotle. . . . Likewise Gerard said a man ought not to be disturbed about any affair of this world. . . . Before all things study specially to be humble inwardly. The knowledge of all knowledge is for a man to know that he knoweth nothing. The more a man is assured that he is far from perfection, the nearer is he thereto. The beginning of vainglory is to be pleasing to one's self. . . . With whatsoever thoughts a man doth fall asleep, with such doth he awaken; at these times it is well to pray or read some psalms.

Before all things know thy vices and thy passions. Be watchful against temptation and the promptings of thy passions. . . . Reply humbly to them that ask of thee. Avoid women, and beware of looking upon them. It is an ill example to the world to keep no guard over the eyes. . . . Thou oughtest not to speak evil of any, unless it can profit thee or him. . . . I think that the thoughts and promptings which come into our hearts are not under our control, but it is in our power to plant good in the heart by reading, prayer, and meditation until these promptings to what is unlawful are overcome and yield, and by the grace of God do cease. . . . We ought to raise our heart to heaven without ceasing, and to turn again and again to the Holy Scripture. . . . By too great haste devotion is lost. Therefore avoid mere repetitions, and do all things with attention and thought, not from habit only. . . . Worldly knowledge is very alluring; therefore let a man beware that he be not too much attracted thereto; let him earnestly desire to pass over to God by means of such knowledge, and not be satisfied therewith as an end in itself. . . . A man ought to direct all his exercises and studies to the conquest of his passions and weakness, for otherwise he doth profit little thereby. In the hours of common labor stand ever on thy guard, and be careful of much speaking. . . . Never be idle, but be busied with some occupation.

Thomas also copied the letter sent by Amilius van Buren to the brethren at Amersfoort, where Radewijns was then staying. In this letter Amilius told the absent rector about the death of Lubbert ten Bossche, or Lubbert Berner, as Thomas calls him. Thomas adds that Van Buren was sitting beside the dying man: "He [Amilius] carefully kept account of all the edifying words which he heard fall from his lips; and after Lubbert's death he faithfully made record of them, writing them in order in a letter . . . and this letter I have determined to insert here." Not satisfied with that, Thomas also copied the letter composed by Lubbert shortly before his death, together with the answer from Radewijns to the brethren at Deventer. The story of Lubbert's decease is very impressive: "And he answered me, as it were in great amazement: 'Wonderful, wonderful, marvelous, marvelous, yea great and marvelous are the things which I saw when I sat up.' And then he added: 'Call the brethren, call the brethren'; and when I called them, immediately he breathed his last." What is still more remarkable, Thomas copied excerpts from the "devout exercises" of this pious brother. He began with the following sentence: "Thy task shall be to labor to uproot thy vices and to gain virtue."

This is not all. Thomas was the trusted friend of Amilius van Buren, rector of the brethren at Deventer during Radewijns's absence in the summer of the year 1398. Amilius had watched by the bedside of the dying Lubbert ten Bossche. From his mouth Thomas "received many of those good things concerning the virtues of the brethren," which he wrote down in his *Lives of Gerard Groote, Florentius Radewijns, and their Disciples.* Who knows how much more Thomas might have told us, and how many more brief sayings he might have preserved which now are lost? He shows how well he was acquainted with the kind cook: "He made the kitchen a house of prayer, for he knew that God is everywhere. . . . He passed no time unfruitfully, nor for a moment neglected his spiritual exercises." Thomas copied the cook's "devout exercises," most likely from the original itself, so that we owe to his busy hand the preservation of this literary production, together with those of Groote, Radewijns, Ten Bossche, and some other men.

Early in 1398 Thomas à Kempis was living in the old vicarage of Radewijns, and not in the new brethren-house, which was called House of Florentius. "At that time," writes Thomas, "there was no small number of clerks living in the several houses under the rule and discipline of that most devout Father, and following the holy commandments of their Lord, his counsels and precepts, and also at set times toiling at the work of copying books for the schools. . . . At this time by the aid and counsel of Florentius I also took up my abode in this house and continued in the community for about one year, having Arnold as my companion. Here indeed I learned to write, to read the Holy Scriptures and books on moral subjects, and to hear devout discourses. . . . All I was then able to earn I gave for the expenses of the community. . . . As he [Arnold] sat with the boys in school he noted

not their childish clamor, but as the master delivered his lecture he wrote the same on paper and
afterward read it over to himself or with a com-
rade. . . . At this time the disciples and most
devout pupils of our beloved father Florentius,
whose lives I have written above, were still in the
flesh, namely, Lubbert, Henry [Brune], Gerard
[Zerbolt], Amilius, James [of Vianen], and John
Ketel, and there were with them some others who
had been amongst the first members of the community," in other words, among the Twelve of
Groote himself.

What was more stimulating still, Radewijns,
whom Thomas had now known for six years, felt
that he was about to die. Many a time he sent
Thomas to the sisters in Groote's old home to ask
them to pray for him, and Thomas also served as
his personal attendant in other ways. Although
Radewijns did not die until 1400, often it seemed as
if death would snatch him away long before the
close of the year 1399. How often must not Thomas
have been called to the bedside of the sick rector!
And the latter, more intent than ever on things
spiritual, cannot have refrained from filling his
pupil's mind with spiritual thoughts. It is no wonder that to Thomas à Kempis we owe the best
biographies of Groote, Radewijns, and Zerbolt.
Moreover, the words of a dying man, or of one who
believes he is dying, are always doubly impressive;
they are always retained longest. On the works of
Zerbolt and Ketel the breath of newly departed
spirits lay fresh and magnetic; here the books of
Groote, the founder, were passed from hand to
hand; here Thomas found all the *rapiaria*, or ex-

cerptbooks, of the leaders, who had lived and labored in the brethren-house. In this house Thomas also found or wrote the Latin book composed by some one whose name the sources do not reveal, at least not in connection with the piece itself, for it seems to have disappeared very soon. This unknown work, very probably drawn up at Deventer by one or more brethren living in the vicarage of Radewijns, we know that Thomas à Kempis copied at Mount St. Agnes between 1416 and 1420, adding some chapters himself; and that it was copied almost immediately in many other monasteries and brethren-houses. Soon it became widely known as the *De Imitatione Christi*, or *Imitation of Christ*.

Scholars interested in the authorship of the *Imitation* are indebted to Dr. Paul Hagen, assistant librarian in the City Library of Lübeck, Germany, for a number of important discoveries he made in that library. When the present writer visited Dr. Hagen at Lübeck, the latter gave him some valuable information, explaining to him how he had conducted his researches. The following deductions are the result.

Among the numerous manuscripts in the City Library at Lübeck which originally belonged to the Sisters of the Common Life of that city, there are two which contain a treatise in Low German called *Admonitions Tending to Things Internal*. Also, there is a manuscript in the same library in which Chapters VI-IX of the fourth book of the *Imitation* are found, all in the same Low-German dialect apparently in use at Lübeck in the fifteenth century. This was not left by the Sisters of the

Page from Manuscript Theologia Germanica no. 15 of the City Library in Lübeck, Germany. It is folio 59v, and corresponds to a part of Chapter VI, book III, of the "Imitation."

Common Life living in the convent of Michael,
but by the Beguines in the "Johanneshof," a house
situated near that of the Sisters of the Common
Life. There can be no doubt that these Beguines
got this literary material from their friends across
the street, and that the latter, in turn, had received
it from one of the sister-houses of Deventer or
Westphalia, for it was the Low Countries that pro-
vided those pious women at Lübeck with religious
productions of various kinds. Just as Thomas à
Kempis was only one of the many boys who received the teachings of Groote's followers at Deventer, and just as the works he wrote had been
preceded by a great many others, so did the sixty-
four chapters of the *Imitation,* translated at Deventer and adapted for the use of the sisters at Lübeck,
form merely a small portion of the writings produced originally at Deventer and spread abroad
by the disciples of Gerard Groote.

The sixty-four chapters in the Low-German
dialect, which we shall call L, were put together
by Thomas à Kempis when he was still living at
Deventer. Now, L differs so much from the other
chapters of Books III and IV that they must have
been written by two different personalities and at
different times, even though the whole work seems
after all to have been compiled by Thomas à
Kempis, as will be shown presently. We find, for
example, that in the first twelve chapters in L the
word "oh" occurs but once. In the first sixty
chapters of L we find it but nine times; but in
the few passages missing here and found in the
complete *Imitation* it occurs thirty times. It is
well known that Thomas à Kempis in his later life

was in the habit of using this interjection. The almost complete absence of the interjection in the L chapters proves that these were written during the last year spent by Thomas at Deventer, where he was so strongly influenced by the lives and ideals of Radewijns. The interjections used by Thomas à Kempis are often followed by rhetorical questions. Such questions rarely occur in L. Thus we read in Chapter XXI of Book III of the *Imitation* proper: "Oh, when shall it be fully granted me, to consider in quietness of mind and see how sweet thou art, my Lord God?" And in Chapter XXXIV: "Oh, when will that blessed and desired hour come?" In Chapter XLVIII no fewer than ten such questions succeed each other, of which the first and last start with "oh, when," and the others with "when." Rhetorical questions are very often repeated in other works by Thomas à Kempis, as, in his *Valley of Lilies,* where, in Chapter XXVI, eight similar questions are found, with the word "oh," in six, and the word "when" in eight. Rhetorical repetitions are also characteristic of Thomas à Kempis's own style. When the writer of the L chapters repeats a word as he repeats "in the cross" nine times in Chapter XII of the second book of the *Imitation,* it is because this is strictly necessary; when Thomas à Kempis repeats, as in using "many" in Book III, Chapter XLVIII, he does so rhetorically. A second example of this sort of repetition, which the L chapters do not have, can be found in Book III, Chapter XXI, where "above all" occurs eighteen times, and in addition the word "thou" is used seven times, the word "alone" six times. Here eleven superlatives are employed. Again, that part of Book III, Chapter LVIII, which has the word "I" sixteen times in a series, is not a part of the L chapters.

The difference in style between the L chapters and those added by Thomas à Kempis is further illustrated by the manner in which God is invoked. While L has only nine comparatively short titles by which to invoke God, the whole *Imitation* has forty-one, some of which are quite elaborate and rhetorical. It is worth noting also that every one of the titles found in the *Imitation,* but absent in L, repeatedly occurs in the other writings of Thomas à Kempis. He undoubtedly was the person who worked over the Latin equivalent of L, adding the customary interjections, questions, and exclamations, so characteristic of his own works. The material he found at Deventer in the year 1398-99 is simpler in style, and far more powerful than the paragraphs which he added on Mount St. Agnes.

One can also prove that the matter which was added to L was added by a young monk. In 1416 Thomas à Kempis was a young monk. He was *the* young monk who wrote that "the life of a good monk is a cross," and that once having proceeded, it will not do for him to look behind him. The author of L, on the contrary, must have been a man of ripe experience outside of a monastery. Apparently he had not been a monk in his previous life, or at least not for a long period. Thomas himself wrote especially for monks, as the contents of Book III, Chapter X, plainly indicate, while L was not addressed to monks only, but to all Christians generally. He who wrote L, even if he was a monk, which appears very doubtful, nowhere so enthusiastically praises monasticism as Thomas à Kempis does. Thomas writes in Chapter X of Book III: "For it is not granted all to forsake all, to renounce the world, and to undertake a life of religious [monastic] retiredness. . . . O sacred state of religious [monastic] servitude." . . . In Chapter LVI we read: "Truly the life of a good monk is a cross"; this same sentence is also found in Vol. IV of his *Opera*, p. 249.

In the use of dialogue the writer of L far surpasses Thomas à Kempis. In L the Lord is the principal speaker, and he is not interrupted by approbation, whereas, in those chapters of Book III not found in L, the author, who is Thomas à Kempis himself, often breaks into the dialogue, and in a wholly unwarranted and inartistic fashion, just as he does in Vol. V of his *Opera,* on pp. 146-150. There he at first addresses Christ, and then speaks to Jesus, Pilate, the reader, and humanity in general, after which he turns to Christ once more. In L the Lord affirms the words of his Son with a short "It is so, my Son" (Chapter XII of Book III); whereas in the *Imitation* we read, "O Lord, it is true," in which the author injects his own personality (Book III, Chapter IV, of which this part is lacking in L), and, "O Lord, what thou sayest is true" (in Book III, Chapter XVII; also lacking in L). In a similar way Thomas throws in some remarks of his own, thus interrupting the Lord, in Book III, Chapter XXIII, "O Lord, do as thou sayest, for this is delightful for me to hear," just as he does in Vol. I of his *Opera,* on p. 4, "Thou hast well said, Lord," and in Vol. IV, on

p. 199, "O Lord, it is true what thou sayest: all that thou sayest pleases me."

When one comes to analyze the subject-matter of L, one sees that Chapters I-XII, XIII-LX, and LXI-LXIV form three independent and original treatises. They are not dependent on the chapters which follow them in the *Imitation* proper. Chapters I-XII of L correspond to Book II of the *Imitation,* which Thomas himself treated as a separate piece of work with a title of its own. Chapters XIII-LX are like forty-eight chapters of Book III, and the way in which they close proves that here the original treatise, called, *Of Internal Consolation,* ends. In L Chapters I-LX appear like one treatise, beginning with the celebrated saying of Christ: "The kingdom of heaven is within you." They close with the following sentence: "Give me a happy departure from this world, and lead me straightway into the kingdom. Amen." They begin and finish with "the kingdom of heaven." Thomas spoiled this fitting end by adding some material of his own, and by changing the order of some of the chapters. The same can be said of Chapters LXI-LXIV of L, which also form an independent treatise with a title and a fitting close. They constitute the best part of Book IV of the *Imitation;* in form and contents they can be easily distinguished from the preceding and following chapters of Book IV. Their title is, *A Short and Fitting Exercise for the Communion Service,* which "exercise" forcibly reminds us of the religious exercises, or *devota exercitia,* of the men at Deventer who left Thomas à Kempis in possession of their literary productions.

The chapters discovered in Lübeck (the L chapters) enable us to restore the original text of the whole *Imitation.* In doing this one can correct mistakes made by Thomas à Kempis in copying the treasures he brought from Deventer. In Book II, Chapter X, of the *Imitation* we read for example: "Semper enim debetur gratia digne gratias referenti: et auferetur ab elato quod dari solet humili." The word *debetur* cannot possibly be correct. The disciples of Groote at Deventer, in common with most theologians in Europe at that time, believed that "grace" was always freely bestowed, and never earned by any mortal being. Not one of them would ever have said that grace ought to be given to anybody, as if God was obliged to give it as a sort of payment. When Thomas came to this place he probably found the word in question in an abbreviated form, as very many words were abbreviated in his day. The original certainly did not have *debetur,* but *dabitur.* Thus we read in Matthew XIII, 12: "Quia enim habet, dabitur ei, et abundabit: qui autem non habet, et quod habet auferetur ab eo." What does L have here? For *debetur* we find *Wet Gheven,* or "it will be given," which is the equivalent of the Latin *dabitur.*

In Book IV, Chapter IX, we read: "Offero quoque tibi omnia pia desideria devotorum: necessitates parentum, amicorum, fratrum, sororum, omniumque carorum meorum." The word *amicorum* cannot be in its right place here, for who would ever think of saying: "My parents, friends, brothers, sisters, and all my dear ones (friends)?" The author must have said: "My parents, brothers, sisters, and all my friends (or dear ones, which means friends)." Hence we read in L: "My parents, brothers, sisters, and all my dear friends." Thomas mistook the word *meorum* for *amicorum*, and the original must have been: "Necessitates parentum meorum, fratrum, sororum, omniumque carorum meorum." Two copies of the *Imitation* have already been found which have *meorum* instead of *amicorum*, and more will doubtless be produced later on. It can also be proved that most of the chapters in Book IV of the *Imitation* were composed by Thomas à Kempis and that he may have found one other short treatise corresponding to Chapters X, XII, XV, and XVIII of this book, and still another or others which were transformed into Book I.

The first book of the *Imitation* actually consists of three distinct parts. The first part (Chapters I-XVI) was addressed to all Christians generally and is by far the best part of the first book, if not of the whole *Imitation*. The second part (Chapters XVII-XXIII) was intended only for Brethren of the Common Life and for members of the Congregation of Windesheim. The title of its first chapter is: "Of the Monastic Life." Many editors changed this title to suit their tastes, but in reality such a change is nothing less than mutilation. At the end of this second part we find the word "Amen," thus showing plainly that here a distinct part is finished. The third part was also intended for monks and Brethren of the Common Life. The word "religious," which frequently occurs in the second and third parts, should as a rule be interpreted "monastic," or else it refers to the status of the Brethren of the Common Life.

The first and second books of the *Imitation* differ in many ways from the other two books. Thomas à Kempis does not seem to have made any important changes in the first two books. For this reason they are reproduced in their entirety. The additions made by him in the third and fourth books are of such an inferior character that in the present edition they have been omitted. Any serious reader will note at once that the *Imitation* won its fame in spite of the additions of à Kempis. His autograph copy in the Royal Library at Brussels plainly shows how he went to work in changing various chapters. In Chapter XI of the second book he inserted at first: "Et si Iesus vellet quod irent in infernum, ibi eque contenti essent nec minimum curarent." He was writing about the lovers of Jesus, and added this strong passage, stating that they would not mind it if Jesus should want them to go to hell. Later he must have repented of this addition, and struck it out with his own hand. The changes he made in the third and fourth books are of a much more innocent nature. One need not feel, however, that one commits sacrilege in eliminating the additions made by A Kempis. The *Imitation* proper was produced in the house of the Brethren of the Common Life in Deventer. In this house all the great mystical productions of the Devotio Moderna originated. In this city Groote had lived and died. Here Thomas à Kempis himself imbibed the teachings of the great master, and here he found the writings of Groote and his disciples, as he testified himself.

Many scholars in Holland and Germany, both Protestant and Roman Catholic, have recently come to the conclusion that the *Imitation of Christ* contains the teachings of Groote in the same way as the four Gospels in the New Testament contain the sayings of Jesus of Nazareth. If Thomas à Kempis merely copied several treatises at Deventer, then he must have copied the writings of Groote alone or of Groote and his immediate followers. If Radewijns, who succeeded Groote at Deventer, dictated to A Kempis, he must have repeated the words of Groote. At any rate the real creator of the *Imitation,* according to the latest theories, is Gerard Groote of Deventer, founder of the Brethren of the Common Life, teacher of Radewijns, and originator of the religious revival named Devotio Moderna. The version of the *Imitation* which follows here is much superior to all the standard editions, and more faithfully represents the teachings of Groote and the principles of his earliest followers, namely, the twelve disciples, of whom one became a traitor,[4] and the apostles who carried the seeds of the new faith across the Continent and into Great Britain and the New World.

4—This is not Thomas à Kempis. For further particulars, see *The Christian Renaissance,* by the same author.

CONTENTS

THE FIRST BOOK

Admonitions Useful for a Spiritual Life

THE SECOND BOOK

ADMONITIONS TENDING TO THINGS INTERNAL

THE THIRD BOOK

OF INWARD CONSOLATION

THE FOURTH BOOK

A DEVOUT EXHORTATION TO THE HOLY COMMUNION

THE FIRST BOOK

ADMONITIONS USEFUL FOR A SPIRITUAL LIFE

CHAPTER I

*Of the Imitation of Christ, and Contempt of All the
Vanities of the World*

E that followeth me, walketh not in darkness," [1] says the Lord.

These are the words of Christ, by which
we are admonished how we ought to imi-
tate his life and ways; if we would be truly enlightened, and be delivered from all blindness of heart.

Let therefore our most earnest study be, to meditate upon the life of Jesus Christ.

The teaching of Christ surpasses all the teachings
of holy men, and he who has his spirit, will find
therein the hidden manna.[2]

But it happens that many who often hear the
Gospel, yet feel but little longing after it, because
they have not the spirit of Christ.

He, therefore, that would fully and with true
wisdom understand the words of Christ, must strive
to conform his whole life to that of Christ.

What does it profit you to dispute profoundly of
the Trinity, if you lack humility and be displeasing
to the Trinity?

Surely it is not deep words that make a man holy
and just, but a virtuous life makes him dear to God.

1—John, VIII, 12.
2—Revelation, II, 17.

I had rather feel contrition than understand the definition thereof.

If you knew the whole Bible by heart,[3] and the sayings of all the philosophers, what would that profit you without the love of God and grace?

Vanity of vanities, all is vanity,[4] save to love God and to serve him only.

This is the highest wisdom, by contempt of the world to reach forward to the heavenly kingdom.

It is vanity then to seek after perishable riches, and to trust in them.

It is also vanity to covet honors, and to lift up ourselves on high.

It is vanity to follow the desires of the flesh, and to labor for that which will afterward bring heavy punishment.

It is vanity to desire a long life, and to have little care for a good life.

It is vanity to take thought only for the present life, and not to look forward to those things which are to come.

It is vanity to love that which quickly passes away, and not to hasten thither where everlasting joy abides.

Call often to mind that proverb: "The eye is not satisfied with seeing, nor the ear with hearing."[5]

Strive, therefore, to wean your heart from visible things, and turn yourself to the invisible.

3—Thomas a Kempis has, "Si *scires* totam bibliam *exterius.*" *Scire exterius* is a literal translation of the Dutch phrase *van buiten kennen*, and is in itself sufficient proof that the Imitation in its original form must have been composed in the Netherlands.

4—Ecclesiastes, I, 2.

5—Verse 8.

For they who follow after their fleshly lusts, defile their conscience, and lose the favor of God.

CHAPTER II
*Of Thinking
Humbly of
One's Self*

Every man naturally desires to know, but what does knowledge avail without the fear of God?

Better indeed is a humble peasant who serves God than a proud philosopher who watches the stars and neglects the knowledge of himself.

He who knows himself well is vile in his own sight, and does not delight in the praises of men.

If I knew all the things in the world, and were not in charity; what would that help me before God, who will judge me according to my deeds?

Rest from inordinate desire of knowledge, for therein is found much distraction and deceit.

Those who have knowledge wish to appear learned and to be called wise.

There are many things the knowledge of which is of little or no profit to the soul.

And he is very unwise who is intent on other things than those which serve the safety of his soul.

Many words do not satisfy the soul, but a good life refreshes the mind; and a pure conscience gives great confidence toward God.

The more you know and the better you know, the more severely you will be judged, unless your life be more holy.

Be not therefore extolled in your own mind for any skill or knowledge of your own, but rather fear for the knowledge intrusted to you.

If it seems to you that you know much and understand things well, know also that there are many more things which you do not know.

Be not high-minded, but rather confess your ignorance.

Why do you desire to lift yourself above another, since there are many more learned and more skilled in the Scripture than you?

If you wish to learn anything with profit, desire to be unknown and to be counted for nothing.

This is the highest and most profitable lesson: the true knowledge and consideration of one's self.

To account nothing of one's self, and to think always well and highly of others, this is great and perfect wisdom.

If you should see another openly sin, or commit some heinous offense, you should nevertheless not reckon yourself any better; for you know not how long you will be able to remain in good estate.

We are all frail, but you ought to hold no one more frail than yourself.

CHAPTER III
Of the Doctrine of Truth

Happy is he whom Truth by itself teaches, not by figures and transient words, but as it is in itself.[6]

Our judgment and senses often deceive us, and they discern but little.

What does it avail to cavil much about dark and hidden things, concerning which we shall not be reproved in the day of judgment, because we did not know them?

It is a great folly to neglect the things that are profitable and necessary, and to give our minds to things which are curious and hurtful.

6—Psalms, XC, 12; Numbers, XII, 8.

We have eyes and see not; and what have we to do with *genus* and *species?*

He to whom the eternal word speaks, is delivered from many theories.

From this One Word are all things, and all things speak of him; and this is the Beginning, which also speaks to us.

No man without that Word understands or judges rightly.

He to whom all things are one, he who reduces all things to one, and sees all things in one, is able to remain steadfast in spirit, and at rest in God.

O God, who art the truth, make me one with thee in everlasting love!

It wearies me often to read and hear many things; in thee is all that I would wish for and desire.

Let all the doctors hold their peace, let all creatures be silent in thy sight; speak thou alone to me.

The more a man is united within himself, and becomes simple inwardly, so much the more and higher things does he understand without labor; because he receives intellectual light from above.

A pure, simple, and steadfast spirit, though employed in many works, is not distracted; because it does all things to the honor of God, and strives to be free from all thoughts of self.

What hinders and troubles you more than the unmortified affections of your own heart?

A good and devout man arranges beforehand within his own heart those things which he is to do outwardly.

Neither do they draw him according to the desires of an evil inclination, but he subjects them to prescript of right reason.

Who has a greater combat than he that strives for mastery of self?

And this ought to be our endeavor, to master self; and daily to grow stronger, and to advance on the better path.

All perfection in this life has some imperfection mixed with it, and all our knowledge is not without some darkness.

A humble knowledge of self is a surer way to God than a deep search after learning.

Not that learning is to be blamed, nor the mere knowledge of anything that is good in itself and ordained by God; but a good conscience and a virtuous life are always to be preferred.

And because many endeavor rather to get knowledge than to live well, therefore they are often deceived, and bear little or no fruit.

Oh, if they would use the care they spend upon their questions, in rooting out their vices and planting virtues, neither would there so much hurt be done, nor so great scandal be caused among the people, nor so much laxity be practised in monasteries.

Truly, in the day of judgment we shall not be asked what we have read, but what we have done; not how well we have spoken, but how virtuously we have lived.

Tell me, where are all those doctors and masters with whom you were well acquainted while they lived and flourished in learning? [7]

Now others possess their prebends and I cannot tell whether they ever think of them.

7—This passage seems to be the work of Groote.

In their lifetime they seemed to be something, but now no one ever speaks of them.

Oh, how quickly passes the glory of the world!

Would that their lives had balanced with their learning; for then they would have studied and read to good purpose.

How many perish through vain learning in this world, who take little care in serving God!

And because they rather choose to be great than to be humble, therefore they have become vain in their imaginations.

He is truly great who has great love.

He is truly great who is little in himself, and counts all height of honor as nothing.

He is truly wise who accounts all earthly things as dung, that he may gain Christ.

And he is truly learned who does the will of God and lets his own will go.

CHAPTER IV
Of Prudence in Action

Not every word or feeling is to be trusted, but a matter should be weighed with caution and patience, as it is with God.

Alas! we often more readily believe and speak evil of others than good: so weak we are.

But perfect [8] men do not easily believe every news-bearer, for they know that human frailty is prone to evil, and apt to fail in words.

It is great wisdom not to be rash in one's actions, nor to be stubborn in his opinions.

It is a part of wisdom, too, not to believe every

8—Perfect men are men who are devout men, not sinless men.

word one hears, nor presently to relate to others what one has heard or does believe.

Consult with him who is wise and conscientious, and seek to be instructed by one better than yourself, rather than follow your own inventions.

A good life makes a man wise before God, and gives him experience in many things.

The more humble a man is in himself, and the more subject unto God, the wiser will he be in all things, and the more at peace.

CHAPTER V
Of the Reading of Holy Scriptures

It is truth, not eloquence, which must be sought for in Holy Scripture.

All Scripture ought to be read in the spirit in which it was written.

We should rather seek for profit in the Scriptures than subtility of speech.

Hence we should read simple and devotional books as willingly as deep and difficult ones.

Let not the authority of the writer offend you, whether he be of great or small learning, but let the love of pure truth draw you to read.

Do not ask who has said this or that, but mark what was said.

Men pass away, but the truth of the Lord remains forever.

God speaks to us in different ways without respect of persons.

Our own curiosity often hinders us in the reading of the Scriptures, when we seek to understand and discuss where we simply should pass on.

If you would reap profit, read with humility, simplicity, and faith; nor ever desire the reputation of learning.

Inquire willingly, and hear in silence the words of holy men; nor be displeased at the parables of older men, for they are not told without cause.

CHAPTER VI
Of Inordinate Affections
Whenever one desires a thing inordinately, he is at once restless within himself.

The proud and avaricious are never at rest; the poor and humble in spirit abide in much peace.

The man who is not yet perfectly dead to himself, is quickly tempted and overcome in trifling things.

He that is weak in spirit, and in a way slave to the flesh and inclined to the pleasures of sense, can hardly withdraw himself altogether from earthly desires.

And therefore he is often afflicted when he does withdraw himself; and is easily angered when opposition is made to him.

Yet if he yield to his inclination, he is immediately weighed down by the condemnation of his conscience; because he followed his passion, which did not help him secure the peace he sought.

True peace of heart is found in resisting passions, not in yielding to them.

There is then no peace in the heart of a carnal man, nor in him who is given to outward things; but in the spiritual and fervent man.

CHAPTER VII
Of Fleeing from Vain Hope and Pride
Vain is he who puts his trust in man or creatures.

Be not ashamed to serve others for the love of Jesus Christ, nor to be reckoned poor in this life.

Do not lean upon yourself, but place your hope in God.

Do what lies in your power, and God will assist you in your good intention.

Do not trust in your learning, nor the cleverness of any living thing, but rather in the grace of God, who helps the humble and humbles the proud.

Do not glory in riches if you have them, nor in friends because powerful, but in God who gives all things, and desires above all things to give himself.

Do not pride yourself on height of stature or beauty of body, which only a slight illness will disfigure and destroy.

Take no pleasure in your skill or wit, lest you displease God, to whom belongs all the good whatsoever that you have.

Do not esteem yourself better than others, lest perchance you appear worse in the sight of God, who knows what is in man.

Be not proud of your good works, for the judgment of God differs from that of men; and what often displeases him, pleases them.

If there be any good in you, believe that there is more in others, so that you may preserve your humility.

It is no harm to you to place yourself below all others, but it does great harm to place yourself above even one.

Peace is ever with the humble, but in the heart of the proud is envy and frequent indignation.

CHAPTER VIII
*Of Shunning
Too Much
Familiarity*

You must not lay open your heart to every one, but tell your case to one who is wise and fears God.

Be seldom with young people and with strangers.

Do not flatter the rich, and do not willingly associate with the great.

Keep company with the humble and the simple, with the devout and the gentle, and discuss subjects which edify.

Be not familiar with any woman, but commend all good women alike to God.

Desire to be familiar with God alone and his angels, and avoid the acquaintance of men.

We must have charity toward all, but familiarity is not expedient.

Sometimes it happens that a person unknown to us is highly regarded because of the good report given by others; whose actual personality is nevertheless unpleasing to those who see him.

We sometimes think to please others by our intimacy, and we rather displease them forthwith by the bad qualities they discover in us.

CHAPTER IX
*Of Obedience
and Subjection*

It is a very great thing to live in obedience, to be under a superior, and not to be a law unto one's self.

It is much safer to obey than to govern.

Many are in obedience from necessity rather than from love, and they are in trouble and easily repine.

Neither do they attain the freedom of mind, unless with all their heart they subject themselves for the love of God.

Go where you will, you will find no rest save in humble subjection to the rule of a superior.

Fancies about places and change have deceived many.

It is true that every one gladly does that which agrees with his own taste, and is more inclined to those who are of his own mind.

But if God is among us, it is necessary that we sometimes relinquish our opinion for the sake of peace.

Who is so wise that he can fully know all things?

Do not therefore trust too much in your own opinion, but be willing to hear the opinion of others.

If what you think is good, and you forgo it for the love of God and follow another, you will profit more thereby.

I have often heard it said: It is safer to hear counsel than to give it.

It may also happen that each one's opinion may be good; but to refuse to yield to others when reason or occasion require it, is a sign of pride and wilfulness.

CHAPTER X
*Of Avoiding
Superfluity
of Words*

Shun as far as you can the tumult of men; for the talk of worldly affairs, though sincerely undertaken, is a hindrance.

For we are quickly defiled and enslaved by vanity.

Many a time I wish I had held my peace, and had not gone among men.

But why do we so gladly speak and gossip, when we seldom return to silence without hurt of conscience?

We do because, by discoursing one with another,

we seek to receive comfort from each other, and desire to ease our minds wearied by sundry thoughts.

And we very willingly talk and think of those things which we most love and desire, or of those which we most dislike.

But alas, often in vain and to no purpose. For this outward consolation is no small detriment to inward and divine consolation.

Therefore we must watch and pray that time pass not idly away.

If it be lawful and expedient to speak, say those things which may edify.

Evil custom and neglect of our profit tend to give much liberty to inconsiderate speech.

Nevertheless devout conversation on spiritual things fosters not a little our spiritual growth, especially when persons of one mind and spirit be gathered together in God.

CHAPTER XI
*Of Gaining
Peace and of
Zealous Desire
of Progress*
We might enjoy much peace if we would not busy ourselves with the words and deeds of other men, which do not concern ourselves.

How long can he abide in peace who meddles in another's affairs, who seeks external cares, who little or seldom concentrates his inner thoughts?

Blessed are the single-hearted, for they will enjoy much peace.

Why were some of the saints so perfect and contemplative?

Because they strove to mortify themselves wholly from all earthly desires; and therefore they could with their whole heart cling to God, and be free to concentrate their inner thoughts.

We are too much occupied with our passions, and too solicitous about transitory things.

We also seldom overcome any one vice perfectly, and are not zealous for daily growth; hence we remain cold and lukewarm.

If we were perfectly dead to ourselves, and not entangled within our own breasts; then should we be able to taste divine things, and to have experience of heavenly contemplation.

The whole and greatest impediment is that we are not freed from our passions and lusts; neither do we strive to enter the perfect way of the saints.

When even a small adversity befalls us, we are too quickly dejected, and turn to human consolations.

If we endeavored like men of courage to stand in the battle, we should feel the help of the Lord upon us from heaven.

For he is ready to aid those who fight and trust in his grace; he provides for us the occasions for fighting in order that we may win the victory.

If we think that progress in religion consists in external observances, our devotion will quickly be at an end.

But let us lay the ax to the root, that, being cleansed from passions, we may find rest to our souls.

If each year we would root out one vice, we should soon become perfect men.

But often we find it just the opposite, namely, that we were better and purer at the beginning of our conversion than after many years of profession.

Fervor and progress should increase daily, but now it is accounted a great achievement, if one can retain part of his first zeal.

If we could put some stress on ourselves at the beginning, we should afterward be able to do all things with ease and joy.

It is hard to break a habit, but harder still to go contrary to one's will.

If you do not overcome little and easy things, how shall you overcome harder things?

Resist your inclination at the beginning and unlearn an evil habit, lest it lead you gradually into a worse difficulty.

Oh, if you considered how much inward peace to yourself and joy to others your holy life would bring, I suppose you would be more anxious for spiritual progress.

CHAPTER XII
Of the Profit of Adversity
It is good for us that we sometimes have troubles and adversities, for they often make a man enter into himself, and consider that he is here in banishment, and ought not to place his trust in any worldly thing.

It is good that we sometimes endure contradictions and are wrongly and unfairly judged, though we do and intend well.

These things often help attain humility, and shield us from vainglory.

For then we rather seek God for our inward witness, when outwardly we are vilified by men and when no credit is given to us.

Therefore a man ought to rest so fully on God that he need not seek many consolations from men.

When a man of good character is afflicted, tempted, or troubled with evil thoughts, then he understands better the great need he has of God, without whom he can do nothing that is good.

Then also he sorrows, laments, and prays, because of the miseries he suffers.

Then he is weary of living longer, and wishes that death would come, that he might be dissolved and be with Christ.

Then also he fully realizes that in this world full peace and perfect safety cannot long abide.

CHAPTER XIII
Of Resisting Temptations

So long as we live in this world we cannot be without tribulation and temptation.

Wherefore it is written in Job: "The life of man upon earth is a trial." [9]

Every one therefore ought to be careful about his temptations, and to watch in prayer, lest the devil find occasion to deceive him; who never sleeps, but goes about seeking whom he may devour.

No man is so perfect and holy that he has not sometimes temptations, and altogether without them we cannot be.

Nevertheless temptations are often very profitable to us, though they be troublesome and grievous, for in them a man is humbled, purified, and instructed.

All the saints passed through temptations and profited.

And those who could not bear temptation became reprobate, and fell away.

There is no order so holy, nor place so secret, where there are no temptations or adversities.

There is no man that is altogether free from temptations while he lives on earth, for in ourselves is the root thereof, being born with an inclination to evil.

9—Job. VII, 1.

When one temptation or tribulation goes away, another comes; and we shall always have something to suffer, because we have lost the blessing of our happy estate.[10]

Many seek to fly from temptations, and fall more deeply into them.

We cannot overcome by flight alone, but by endurance and true humility we are made stronger than all our enemies.

He who only resists them outwardly, and does not pluck them out by the roots, will profit little.

Nay, temptations will return to him more quickly, and he will be in a worse plight.

Little by little and through patience with longsuffering, you will conquer by the help of God rather than by violence and your own importunity.

Often take counsel in temptation, and do not deal harshly with him who is tempted; but give him comfort, as you would wish to be done to yourself.

The beginning of all evil temptations is inconstancy of mind, and little trust in God. For as a ship without a helm is tossed to and fro with the waves, so the man who is careless and infirm of purpose is tempted in many ways.

Fire tries iron, and temptation a just man.

We often do not know what we can do, but temptation reveals what we are.

Nevertheless the beginning of a temptation must be watched, for the enemy is then the more easily overcome, if he is not allowed to enter the door of our hearts, but is resisted outside the door as soon as he has knocked.

10—Paradise.

Wherefore some one said, "Check the beginnings, else the remedy will be too late."

For first there comes to the mind a bare thought, then a strong imagination, afterward pleasure, evil affection, assent.

And so little by little the enemy enters completely, since he was not resisted at the beginning.

And the longer one postpones resistance, the weaker he grows each day, and his enemy stronger against him.

Some suffer great temptations in the beginning of their conversion; others at the end.

Some in fact are troubled throughout their whole lives. Some are easily tempted, according to the wisdom and equity of the divine appointment, which weighs the states and merits of men, and ordains all things for the welfare of his elect.[11]

We ought not therefore to despair when we are tempted, but so much the more fervently pray unto God, that he will vouchsafe to help us in every tribulation, because he will, according to the words of Paul,[12] give the temptation such issue that we shall be able to bear it.

Let us therefore humble our souls under the hand of God in every temptation and tribulation, because he will save and exalt the humble in spirit.

In temptations and afflictions a man is proved how much he has profited; and therein is his reward the greater, and his virtue shines forth the more.

Neither is it a great thing if a man be devout and fervent, when he feels no affliction; but if in time

11—This passage, in common with many sayings of Groote, contains germs of the doctrine of predestination.

12—I Corinthians, X, 13.

of adversity he bear himself patiently, there will be hope of great progress.

Some are kept from great temptations, and in small ones which daily occur are often overcome; in order that, being humbled, they shall not trust themselves in great matters, as they are weak in such small things.

CHAPTER XIV
*Of Avoiding
Rash Judgment*

Turn your eyes unto yourself, and beware you do not judge the deeds of others.

In judging others a man labors in vain, often errs, and easily sins, but in judging and examining himself he always labors fruitfully.

Just as we have a thing at heart, so do we often judge of it, for true judgment we easily lose through personal love.

If God were always the pure intention of our desire, we should not be so easily troubled by the resistance of our feelings.

But often something lurks within or else occurs from without, which draws us after it.

Many secretly seek their own ends in what they do, and know it not.

They seem to live in good peace of mind, when things are done according to their will and opinion. But if things happen otherwise than they desire, they are immediately disturbed and vexed.

Through diversity of judgments and opinions, dissensions frequently arise between friends and countrymen, between religious and devout persons.

An old custom is not easily relinquished, and no one is willingly led beyond his range of vision.

If you rely more on your reason or industry than

on the virtue of subjection to Jesus Christ, you will rarely and slowly become an enlightened man, for God wants us to be perfectly subject to him, and all our reason exalted by burning love.

CHAPTER XV
*Of Works Done
out of Love*

For no worldly thing, and for the love of no man, is any evil to be done; but for the profit of him who is needy, a good work should be freely postponed, or changed also for a better one.

For when this is done, a good work is not destroyed, but improved.

Without love an outward act profits nothing; but whatever is done out of love, no matter how small and of little repute, it will become wholly fruitful.

For God weighs more the motive than the act.

He does much who loves much.

He does much who does a thing well.

He does well who rather serves the community than his own will.

It often seems to be love, and it is rather carnality, because natural inclination, self-will, hope of reward, desire of gain, rarely desire to be away.

He who has true and perfect love seeks his own good in nothing, but desires that in all things only the glory of God be done.

He also envies nobody, because he loves no joys of his own, nor does he want to rejoice in himself, but wishes above all things to be made happy in the enjoyment of God.

He ascribes nothing that is good to any man, but wholly to God, from whom, as from a fountain, all good proceeds, in whom at last all the saints will rest in joy.

Oh, he who has but a spark of love would certainly discern that all earthly things are full of vanity.

CHAPTER XVI
Of Bearing with the Faults of Others

Those things which a man cannot amend in himself or in others, he ought to bear patiently till God shall ordain otherwise.

Think that perhaps it is better so for your trial and patience, without which our merits are worth little.

You should nevertheless pray when you have such impediments, that God may vouchsafe to sustain you, and you may be able to bear them graciously.

If one who is once or twice admonished will not pay heed, do not contend with him, but commit all to God, that his will be done and his honor be shown in all his servants, for he knows well how to turn evil into good.

Strive to be patient in bearing with the defects and infirmities of others, whatsoever they may be, for you yourself have many which other people will have to endure.

If you cannot make yourself such as you wish, how can you expect to have another fashioned to your liking?

We like to have others perfect, and yet we do not amend our faults.

We will that others be severely corrected, and will not be corrected ourselves.

The great liberty of others displeases us, and yet we do not want to deny ourselves what we desire.

We will have others restrained by rules, but we will not suffer to have them restrain us.

Thus it appears how seldom we weigh our neighbor in the same balance with ourselves.

If all men were perfect, what should we have to suffer of our neighbor for God?

But now God has thus ordained that we may learn to bear each other's burdens; for no one is without fault, no one without burden, no one sufficient in himself, no one wise enough in himself; but we must bear with each other, and comfort, help, instruct, and admonish each other.

How much strength each one has, is best shown by the occasions of adversity.

For such occasions do not make a man weak, but reveal what he is.

CHAPTER XVII
*Of the
Monastic Life*

You must learn to break your own will in many things, if you wish to live in peace and concord with others.

It is no small matter to live in a religious community or congregation, and here to converse without complaint, and to persevere faithfully till death.

Blessed is he who lived here a good life and came to a happy end.

If you will persevere and profit as you ought, consider yourself an exile and pilgrim upon the earth.

You must be content for Christ's sake to be esteemed a fool in this world, if you wish to lead a religious life.

The garments and the tonsure are of small account; but change of manners and entire mortification of passions make a truly religious man.

He who seeks anything but purely God and the salvation of his soul shall find nothing but tribulation and misery.

Neither can he remain long in peace who does not try to be the least and subject to all.

You came to serve, not to rule.

You must know that you were called to suffer and to labor, not to idle and gossip.

Here therefore are men tried as gold in the furnace.

Here no one can stand unless he humbles himself with all his heart for God's sake.

CHAPTER XVIII
Of the Examples
of the Holy
Fathers
Consider the vivid patterns of the holy fathers, in whom shone true perfection and religion; and you will see how small it is, and almost nothing, which we do.

Ah! what is our life, if compared to theirs?

The saints and friends of Christ served the Lord in hunger and thirst, in cold and nakedness, in labor and fatigue, in watching and fasting, in saintly prayers and meditations, in persecutions and many insults.

Oh, how many and grievous tribulations they suffered, those apostles, martyrs, confessors, virgins; and all the others who chose to follow in Christ's footsteps!

For they hated their lives in this world, that they might keep them unto life eternal.

Oh, how strict and self-renouncing a life those holy fathers led in the wilderness! what long and grievous temptations they suffered! how often they were assaulted by the enemy! what frequent and fervent prayers they offered to God! what rigid abstinences they endured!

What great zeal and care for spiritual progress

did they manifest! how strong a combat did they have to overcome their lusts! what pure and upright intentions did they keep toward God!

By day they labored, and at night they attended to continual prayer; even when they labored, they did not cease from mental prayer.

They spent all their time with profit; every hour seemed short for the service of God, and by reason of the great sweetness they felt in contemplation, they forgot the necessity of corporal refreshments.[13]

They renounced all riches, dignities, honors, friends, and kinsfolk; they desired to have nothing which appertained to the world; they scarcely took things necessary for the sustenance of life; they grieved to minister to the body even when necessary.

Therefore they were poor in earthly goods, but very rich in grace and virtues; outwardly they were destitute, but inwardly they were refreshed with grace and divine consolation.

They were strangers to the world, but intimate and familiar friends to God.

They seemed to themselves as nothing and to this world contemptible; but in the eyes of God they were precious and beloved.

They remained in true humility; they lived in simple obedience.

They walked in love and patience, and therefore profited daily in spirit; and they obtained great favor before God.

They were given as an example to all religious men, and they should more provoke us to good lives than the number of the lukewarm tempt to a lax life.

13—This is what Groote and Radewijns also did, while Thomas a Kempis enjoyed better food.

Oh, how great was the fervor of all religious persons in the beginning of their holy institution! [14]

Oh, what devotion to prayer! what rivalry in virtue! what strict discipline then observed! what reverence and obedience under the rule of the master then shown!

Their footsteps yet remaining [15] do testify that they were indeed holy and perfect men, who fighting so bravely trod the world under their feet.

Now a man is counted great, if only he be not a transgressor, and who can with patience endure that which he has undertaken.

Oh, the lukewarmness and negligence of our times! that we so quickly decline from the former love, and it has become a weariness to live, because of sloth and lukewarmness.

May progress in holiness not wholly fall asleep in you, who have often seen the many examples of the devout!

CHAPTER XIX
Of the Spiritual Exercises of a Religious Person [16]

The life of a religious person ought to be adorned with all virtues, that he may be inwardly what he appears to be outwardly to men.

And with reason there ought to be much more within than is perceived without, for God is a discerner of our hearts, whom we must reverence most highly wherever we are, and walk pure in his presence as do the angels.

Daily we ought to renew our resolutions, and to

14—Monasticism.

15—This may refer to Groote and those of his disciples who founded the monastery of Windesheim.

16—The term "religious person" usually refers to a member of some brotherhood, either monastic or semi-monastic.

stir up ourselves to fervor, as though this were the first day of our conversion, and to say, "Help me, Lord God, in my good resolution, and in thy holy service, and grant that this day I may make a perfect beginning, for hitherto I have done nothing!"

According to our purpose is the rate of our progress, and much diligence is necessary to him who would make good progress.

For if he who resolves bravely often fails, what will he do who resolves seldom or feebly?

In manifold ways it happens that we leave off our plan, and a trivial omission of spiritual exercises is rarely made without some loss.

The purpose of just men depends not upon their own wisdom, but rather upon the grace of God; for on him they always rely for anything they undertake.

For man proposes, but God disposes; and the way of a man is not in himself.[17]

If an accustomed exercise is sometimes omitted, either for some act of piety or some brotherly kindness, it can easily be resumed afterward.

But if it be neglected through disinclination or slothfulness, then it is sinful and the injury will be felt.

Let us do the best we can, we shall still too easily fail in many things.

Nevertheless some distinct resolution should always be made, and especially against those sins which most easily beset us.

Both our outer and inner life should be diligently examined, because both of them have to do with our progress.

17—Jeremiah. X. 23.

If you cannot continually recollect yourself, do it at any rate sometimes, at least once a day, in the morning or at night.

In the morning form your resolutions, in the evening examine your life, how you have behaved during the day in word, deed, and thought, for in these perhaps you have often offended both God and your neighbor.

Gird up your loins as a man against the evil assaults of the devil; bridle your appetites, and you will soon be able to bridle every inclination of the flesh.

Never be wholly unoccupied, but either be reading, or writing, or praying, or meditating, or doing something useful for the community.

Bodily exercises, however, are to be undertaken with discretion, nor are they to be practised by all men alike.

Those exercises which are not common to all are not to be exposed to the public view, for things private are more safely practised in secret.

Nevertheless take care not to neglect the common exercises nor to be more ready for what is private, but, having wholly and faithfully fulfilled all that is ordered and enjoined on you, if then you have leisure, turn your thoughts upon yourself, as your devotion will desire.

All cannot have one kind of exercise, but one is more useful for this person, another for that.

According to the seasonableness of the times divers exercises are fitting; some suit better for working days, others for holy days.

We need one kind in the time of temptation, and others in time of peace and quietness.

Some we love to practise when we are sad, others when we rejoice in the Lord.

About the time of the chief festivals good exercises are to be renewed, and the prayers of holy men more fervently to be implored.

From festival to festival we ought to make resolutions, as though we were about to depart from this world, and to come to the everlasting feast.

Therefore we ought to prepare ourselves earnestly at holy times, and to live more devoutly, and to keep more strictly every observance, as though we were soon to receive the reward of our labors at the hand of God.

And if this be deferred, let us believe ourselves to be as yet unprepared, and unworthy of the glory which shall be revealed in us in due time; and let us study to prepare ourselves better for our departure.

"Blessed is that servant," says the evangelist Luke, "whom his Lord when he cometh, shall find watching.

"Verily, I say unto you, he shall make him ruler over all his goods." [18]

CHAPTER XX
Of the Love
of Solitude
and Silence

Seek a convenient time to retire into yourself, and meditate often on God's kind deeds.

Leave your curious questions; read such things as bring compunction for sin rather than busy thoughts.

If you will withdraw yourself from useless talk, and idle goings-about, as well as from novelties and gossips, you will find leisure enough and suitable for good meditation.

18—Luke, XII, 43-44.

The greatest saints avoided whenever they could the society of men, and chose to serve God in secret.

One has said, "As often as I have gone among men, I returned home less a man."

This we often find true when we have talked long together.

It is easier to be altogether silent than to say more than we should.

It is easier to remain at home than to keep sufficient guard upon one's self out of doors.

He therefore who seeks to reach the inward and spiritual things must with Jesus depart from the multitude.

No man safely appears abroad unless he gladly remains hidden in the home.

No man speaks securely unless he gladly holds his peace.

No man rules safely unless he is willing to be ruled.

No man commands securely unless he has learned well how to obey.

No man rejoices securely unless he has within himself the testimony of a good conscience.

The security of the saints was always full of the fear of God; neither were they the less earnest and humble in themselves, because they shone outwardly with great virtues and grace.

But the security of bad men arises from pride and presumption, and in the end it turns to their own deception.

Never promise yourself security in this life, even though you seem to be a good monk or a pious hermit.

Often those who were most highly esteemed by men have fallen more grievously because of too much confidence in themselves.

Wherefore to many it is more profitable not to be altogether free from temptations, but to be often assaulted, lest they feel themselves too secure, and so perhaps be puffed up with pride, or else too freely give themselves to worldly comforts.

Oh, how good a conscience would he keep who never sought after transitory joy, nor ever entangled himself with the things of this world!

Oh, how great peace and quiet would he possess who cut off all vain anxiety, and thought only upon divine things and such as were profitable for his soul, and placed all his confidence in God.

No man is worthy of heavenly comfort, unless he has diligently exercised himself in holy compunction.

If you desire contrition of heart, enter into your secret chamber and shut out the tumults of the world, as it is written, "In your chambers be ye grieved." [19]

In your chamber you will find what you often lose abroad.

Retirement, if you continue in it, will grow sweet; but if you do not keep in it, it causes weariness.

If in the beginning of your conversion you are content to remain in it, and keep it well, it will afterward be to you a dear friend, and a most pleasant comfort.

In silence and quiet a devout soul advances and learns the mysteries of Holy Scripture; here it finds rivers of tears, in which it may each night wash and cleanse itself, that it may be the more familiar with

19—Psalms, IV, 4.

its creator, the farther removed it lives from worldly disquiet.

To him who withdraws himself from acquaintances and friends, God with his holy angels will draw nigh.

It is better to live privately and to take care of one's self than to neglect one's self and work wonders.

It is commendable in a religious person rarely to go abroad, to fly from being seen, to have no desire to see men.

Why do you wish to see that which is unlawful for you to have?

The world passes away and the lusts thereof.

The desires of sensuality draw you abroad, but when an hour is past, what do you carry home but a burdened conscience and a distracted heart?

A merry going forth often brings a sorrowful return, and a merry evening makes a sad morning.

So all carnal joy enters gently, but in the end it bites and stings to death.

What can you see elsewhere that you cannot see here?

Behold the heaven and the earth and the elements, for out of these are all things created.

What can you see anywhere that can long continue under the sun?

You think perchance to satisfy yourself, but you will never be able to attain to this.

If you saw all things present before your eyes, what were it but a vain vision?

Lift up your eyes to God in the highest, and pray him to pardon your sins and shortcomings.

Leave vain things to the vain, but be intent upon those things which God has commanded you.

Shut your door upon you and call unto you Jesus, your beloved.

Stay with him in your closet, for you will not find so great peace anywhere else.

If you had not gone abroad and listened to vain talk, you would better have kept yourself in good peace.

But because sometimes it gives you delight to hear new things, you must suffer for it trouble of heart.

CHAPTER XXI
Of Compunction of Heart

If you wish to make any progress, keep yourself in the fear of God, and do not long to be too free; but restrain your senses under discipline and give not yourself over to foolish mirth.

Give yourself to compunction of heart, and you will find devotion.

Compunction opens the way to much good, which dissoluteness is wont to destroy quickly.

It is a wonder that any man can ever perfectly rejoice in this life, if he duly weighs and considers his banishment, and the many perils which beset his soul.

Through lightness of heart and neglect of our shortcomings we do not feel the real sorrows of our souls, and often vainly laugh when we have just cause to weep.

There is no true liberty nor right joy but in the fear of God with a good conscience.

Happy is he who can cast away all distracting impediments, and bring himself to the one purpose of holy compunction.

Happy is he who abandons whatever may defile or burden his conscience.

Resist manfully; one habit overcomes another.

If you know how to let others alone, they will gladly let you alone to do your work.

Do not busy yourself in the affairs of others, nor entangle yourself with the business of your superiors.

Keep always your eye on yourself first, and give advice especially to yourself before all your dearest friends.

If you do not possess the favor of men, be not grieved at it, but take this to heart, that you do not behave yourself so circumspectly as becomes a servant of God and a devout religious man.

It is often better and safer for a man not to have many consolations in this life, especially those which concern the flesh.

But that we have no divine consolations or rarely feel them, is our fault, because we seek not after compunction of heart, nor altogether forsake the vain and worldly comforts.

Know that you are unworthy of divine consolation, and that you have rather deserved many tribulations.

When a man has perfect compunction, then the whole world is burdensome and bitter to him.

A good man finds sufficient cause for mourning and weeping.

For whether he considers himself, or reflects on his neighbor's condition, he knows that no one lives here without tribulations.

And the more thoroughly he considers himself, the more he grieves.

Our sins and vices, wherein we lie so entangled that we seldom are able to contemplate heavenly things, are grounds for just sorrow and inward contrition.

If you thought more frequently of your death than of living long, you would undoubtedly be more zealous to improve.

And if also you would seriously consider the future pains of hell or purgatory, I believe you would willingly undergo any toil or pain in this world, and not be afraid of the greatest austerity.

But because these things do not enter the heart, and we still love pleasant things, therefore we remain cold and very indifferent.

It is often from poverty of spirit that the wretched body so easily complains.

Pray therefore to the Lord with humility that he will give you the spirit of compunction, and say with the prophet, "Feed me, O Lord, with the bread of tears, and give me plenteousness of tears to drink." [20]

CHAPTER XXII
Of the Consideration of Human Misery

Miserable you are wherever you are and wherever you turn, unless you turn yourself to God.

Why are you troubled because things do not happen according to your wishes and desires?

Who is he that has everything to his liking?

Neither I, nor you, nor any other man on earth.

There is no man in the world without some tribulation or perplexity, though he were king or pope.

Who is he who has the happiest lot? Even he who is able to suffer something for God.

Many weak and unstable persons say, "Look what

20—Psalms, LXXX, 5.

a happy life that man leads, how rich and great he is, how powerful and exalted!"

But lift up your eyes to the good things of heaven, and you will see that all the goods of this life are nothing; they are very uncertain and very burdensome because they are never possessed without care and fear.

Man's happiness does not consist in the abundance of temporal goods, but a moderate portion is sufficient for him.

Truly it is misery to live on the earth; the more spiritual a man desires to be, the more bitter does this present life become to him, because he feels better and sees more clearly the defects of human corruption.

For to eat, to drink, to watch, to sleep, to rest, to labor, and to be subject to the other necessities of nature is truly a great misery and affliction to a devout man, who would fain be released and free from all sin.

For the inner man is greatly weighed down with the necessities of the body in this world.

Wherefore the prophet devoutly prays to be freed from them, saying, "Deliver me from my necessities, Lord!" [21]

But woe to those who know not their own miseries, and yet greater woe to those who love this miserable and corruptible life!

For to such a degree do some cling to it, that although by labor or by begging they can scarcely procure what is necessary for subsistence, if they might live here always, they would care nothing at all for the kingdom of God.

21—Psalms, XXV, 17.

O senseless and faithless of heart who lie buried so deep in the earth that they can relish nothing save carnal things!

But miserable as they are, they will find out at last to their grief how vile and worthless was that which they loved.

Whereas the saints of God and all the devout friends of Christ did not pay attention to those things which pleased the flesh, nor to those which flourished in this life, but longed after the everlasting riches with their whole hope and earnest intention.

Their whole desire was carried upward to things eternal and invisible, lest they should be drawn downward by the love of visible things.

Lose not, brother, your confidence of making progress in godliness; there is still time, the hour is not past.

Why do you wish to defer your good purpose?

Arise, begin instantly, and say, "Now is the time to be doing, now is the time to fight, now is the proper time for amendment."

When you are ill at ease and troubled, then it is time to be blessed.

You must needs pass through fire and water before you enter the place of refreshing.

Unless you force yourself, you will never overcome sin.

As long as we carry about us this frail body, we can never be without sin or live without weariness and pain.

We would gladly have rest from all misery, but since through sin we have lost our innocence, we have lost also the true happiness.

Therefore we must have patience, and wait for the

mercy of God, until this iniquity passes away, and mortality is swallowed up by life.

Oh, how great is the frailty of man, which is ever prone to evil!

To-day you confess your sins, and to-morrow you commit the very same that you have confessed.

Now you resolve to avoid a fault, and within an hour you behave as if you had resolved nothing.

Good cause we have therefore of humbling ourselves, and never to think highly of ourselves, because we are so frail and unstable.

Besides, quickly may that be lost by our negligence which by much labor we hardly attained through grace.

What will become of us in the end, if we grow lukewarm so early?

Woe to us, if we choose to rest, as though it were a time of peace and security, while as yet there appears no sign of holiness in our conversation.

We have much need to begin afresh, as good novices, to be instructed again to good life, if haply there be some hope of future amendment and greater progress in things spiritual.

CHAPTER XXIII
Of Meditation on Death

Very quickly there will be an end of you here; look what will become of you in another world. To-day man is, and to-morrow he has disappeared.

And when he is out of sight, he is also quickly out of mind.

Oh, the dullness and hardness of man's heart, which thinks only of the present, and does not care more for the future!

You ought so to order yourself in every word and deed, as if to-day you were to die.

If you had a good conscience, you would not greatly fear death.

It is better to avoid sins than to fly from death.

If to-day you are not ready, how will you be so to-morrow?

To-morrow is an uncertain day, and how do you know that you will have a to-morrow?

What does it profit to live long, if we amend so little?

Alas, long life does not always amend, but often increases our guilt.

Oh, that we might spend a single day well in this world!

Many count the years since they were converted, and yet the fruit of amendment is often small.

If it is a dreadful thing to die, it may perhaps be more dangerous to live long.

Happy is he who always has the hour of his death before his eyes, and daily prepares himself to die.

If you have ever seen one die, consider that you also will pass away by the same road.

When it is morning, think that you will not see evening.

And when evening comes, dare not to boast of the next morning.

Be always ready, and live in such a way that death may never take you unprepared.

Many die suddenly and unexpectedly, for "at such an hour as ye think not, the Son of man cometh." [22]

When that last hour comes, you will begin to

22—Matthew, XXIV, 44.

think very differently of your whole past life, and
be exceedingly sorry that you have been so negligent
and slothful.

Oh, how happy and wise is he who now strives
to be such in his life as he wishes to be found at
the hour of death!

A perfect contempt of the world, a fervent desire
to excel in virtue, the love of discipline, the pain-
fulness of repentance, readiness to obey, denial of
self, submission to any adversity for love of Christ—
these are the things which will give us great confidence of a happy death.

While you are in health, you may do much good,
but when you are ill, I see not what you will be
able to do.

Few are made better by sickness, even as they who
wander abroad seldom become holy.

Do not trust to friends and kinsfolk, neither put
off the work of salvation, for men will forget you
sooner than you think.

It is better to provide now in time, and to do
some good beforehand, than to trust to the help of
others.

If you are not careful for yourself now, who will
be careful for you hereafter?

The present time is most precious; "now is the
day of salvation, now is the accepted time."

But alas! that you should spend your time so idly
here, when you might lay up treasure and live
forever.

It will come to pass that you will desire one day
or one hour for amendment, and I cannot say that
you will obtain it.

O beloved, from what danger might you deliver

yourself, from what fear set yourself free, if you would always be fearful and mindful of death!

Strive now so to live that at the hour of death you may rather rejoice than fear.

Learn now to die to the world, that then you may begin to live with Christ.

Learn now to despise all things, that then you may freely go to Christ.

Chastise your body now by penitence, that then you may have a sure confidence.

Ah, foolish one, why do you think that you will live long, when you are not sure of a single day?

How many have been deceived and suddenly snatched away from the body!

How often you hear these reports, how one was slain by the sword, another drowned, another broke his neck by a fall from some high place, another died eating, another when playing; one perished by fire, another by the sword, another by the plague, another slain by a robber; and thus death is the end of all, and the life of man passes away as a shadow.

Who will remember you when you are dead, and who will pray for you?

Work, work now, dearly beloved, work all that you can, because you know not when you are going to die, nor what will befall you after death.

Now while you have time, lay up for yourself everlasting riches.

Think of nothing but your salvation; care for nothing but the things of God.

Make friends for yourself by venerating the saints of God and walking in their steps, that when you fail in this life, they may receive you into ever-lasting habitations.[23]

Keep yourself as a stranger and pilgrim upon the earth, to whom the affairs of this world do not appertain.

Keep your heart free and lifted up to God, because here you have no continuing city.[24]

To him direct your daily prayers and sighs with crying and tears, that after death your spirit may be found worthy to pass happily to the Lord. Amen.

CHAPTER XXIV
*Of Judgment
and the
Punishment
of the Wicked*

In all things remember the end, and how you will stand before a strict judge, from whom nothing is hid, who is not bribed with gifts, nor accepts excuses, but will judge righteous judgment.

O wretched and foolish sinner, what will you answer to God who knows all your wickedness, since you sometimes fear the countenance of an angry man?

Why do you not provide for yourself against that great day of judgment, when no man will be able to excuse or answer for another, but each one will have enough to bear himself?

Now is your labor fruitful, your weeping acceptable, your groaning audible, your sorrow pleasing to God and cleansing to your soul.

The patient man has a great and wholesome purgatory, who when suffering injuries grieves more for the other's malice than for his own wrong, who

23—Luke, XVI, 9.
24—Hebrews, XIII, 14.

prays willingly for his adversaries, and from his heart forgives their offenses, who is not slow to ask pardon from others, who is sooner moved to compassion than to anger, who frequently does himself violence, and tries to bring the flesh wholly into subjection to the spirit.

It is better to purify ourselves from sin and cut off our vices here than to keep them for future purification.

Truly we deceive ourselves through an inordinate love of the flesh.

What is there that the infernal fire will feed upon except your sins?

The more you spare yourself now, and follow the flesh, the more severe will be your punishment hereafter, and the more fuel are you heaping up for the flame.

In the things wherein a man has sinned will he be punished the more severely.

There the slothful will be pricked forward with burning goads, and the glutton tormented with extreme hunger and thirst.

There the luxurious and lovers of pleasure will be bathed in burning pitch and stinking brimstone, and the envious will howl as mad dogs for very grief.

There is no sin which will not be visited with its own proper punishment.

There the proud will be filled with utter confusion and the covetous pinched with miserable poverty.

One hour of pain there will be more bitter than a hundred years of the sharpest penitence here.

There will be no quiet, no comfort for the lost,

though here there is sometimes respite from pain and enjoyment of the comforts of friends.

Be now solicitous and sorrowful, because of your sins, that in the day of judgment you may be secure with the blessed.

For then the righteous will stand with great boldness against those who have vexed and oppressed them.

Then will he stand to judge who now humbly submits himself to the judgment of men.

Then the poor and humble will have great confidence, and the proud will be taken with fear on every side.

Then will it be seen that he was wise in this world who had learned to be a fool and despised for Christ's sake.

Then will every affliction patiently undergone delight us, and the mouth of the ungodly will be closed.

Then every devout man will rejoice, and every profane man will mourn.

Then the afflicted flesh will rejoice more than if it had always been nourished in delights.

Then the lowly garment will put on beauty and the precious robe will seem vile.

Then the poor cottage will be commended more than the gilded palace.

Then will enduring patience give more aid than all worldly power.

Then simple obedience will be exalted above all worldly wisdom.

Then a pure and good conscience will rejoice more than learned philosophy.

Then the contempt of riches will have more weight than all the worldling's treasure.

Then you will find more comfort in having prayed devoutly than in having fared sumptuously.

Then will you rejoice more in having kept silence than in having made long speeches.

Then will good works avail more than fine words.

Then a strict life and severe penitence will be more pleasing than all earthly delights.

Learn now to suffer a little, that then you may be delivered from more grievous pains.

Prove first here what you can endure hereafter.

If now you can endure so little, how will you then be able to bear eternal torments?

If now a little suffering makes you impatient, what will hell-fire do then?

You certainly cannot have two paradises; to enjoy delights in this world and to reign with Christ hereafter.

If until this day you had always lived in honors and delights, what would all that profit you, if you were to die this moment?

All is therefore vanity, except to love God and to serve him only.

For he who loves God with all his heart, fears neither death, nor punishment, nor judgment, nor hell; for perfect love gives sure access to God.

But he who takes delight in sin, what wonder is it if he is afraid both of death and of judgment?

Nevertheless it is a good thing, if love as yet cannot withhold you from evil, that at least the fear of hell should restrain you.

But he who puts aside the fear of God can never continue long in good estate, but will quickly fall into the snares of the devil.

CHAPTER XXV
Of the Zealous Amendment of Our Whole Life

Be watchful and diligent in God's service, and consider frequently whither you have gone and why you have renounced the world.

Was it not that you might live to God and become a spiritual man?

Be fervent then in going forward, for shortly you will receive the reward of your labors; and there will be neither fear nor sorrow within your borders.

Now you will labor but a little, and you will find great rest, yea, perpetual joy.

If you will remain faithful and zealous in action, God will no doubt be faithful and zealous in rewarding you.

You ought to have a good hope that you will attain the victory, but you must not feel secure, lest you grow either negligent or proud.

A certain man, being in anxiety, often wavered between fear and hope, and once, being oppressed with grief, humbly prostrated himself in church before the altar in prayer, and meditated within himself, saying, "Oh! if I knew that I should still persevere."

And presently he heard within him an answer from God, "And if you knew, what would you do?

"Do now what you would do then, and you will be very secure."

And forthwith, being comforted and strengthened, he committed himself wholly to the will of God, and that anxious fluctuation ceased.

Nor did he have a mind to search curiously any further, to know what would befall him, but rather strove to inquire what was the good and acceptable will of God for the beginning and perfecting of every good work.

"Hope in the Lord, and do good," says the prophet, "and inhabit the land, and you will be fed with its riches." [25]

There is one thing which holds many back from spiritual progress, and fervent amendment, namely, extreme fear of the difficulty or of the labor of the combat.

However, they above others improve in virtue who manfully endeavor to overcome those things which are most grievous and contrary to them.

For there a man profits most and obtains greatest grace where he most overcomes himself and mortifies himself in spirit.

But all men have not equally much to overcome and mortify.

Yet he who is diligent will profit more, although he have stronger passions, than another who is of a more temperate disposition, but is less fervent in the pursuit of virtue.

Two things especially aid in the process of great amendment, namely, to withdraw one's self violently from the sin to which nature is viciously inclined, and fervently to labor for that good which one wants most.

Strive also earnestly to guard against and subdue those faults which frequently displease you in others.

Gather some profit to your soul wherever you are, and if you see or hear of good examples, stir yourself to follow them.

But if you observe anything reprehensible, be careful not to do the same.

25—Psalms, XXXVII. 3.

And if at any time you have done it, strive quickly to amend yourself.

As your eye observes others, so in turn you will be noticed by others.

How pleasant and sweet a thing it is to see fervent and devout brothers, who are well mannered and well disciplined!

How sad and grievous it is to see them live dissolute lives, not practising those things to which they were called!

How hurtful it is to neglect the good purpose of their calling, and to turn their minds to that which is not committed to them!

Be mindful of the duties you have undertaken, and keep always before your eyes the remembrance of the Crucified.

You ought to be ashamed indeed as you look upon the life of Jesus Christ, because you have not as yet endeavored to conform yourself more unto him, though you have been a long time in the way of God.

A religious man who exercises himself seriously and devoutly, in the most holy life and passion of our Lord, will here find abundantly whatever is necessary and profitable for him, nor does he need to seek anything better than Jesus.

Oh, if Jesus crucified would come into our hearts, how quickly and completely should we become instructed!

A fervent religious man receives and bears all things well that are commanded him.

But he who is negligent and lukewarm has tribulation upon tribulation, and on all sides is afflicted; because he is without inward consolation, and is forbidden to seek external comforts.

A religious man who is living without discipline is exposed to grievous ruin.

He who seeks easier and lighter rules will ever live in distress, because one thing or another will displease him.

How do so many other religious persons act who are strictly confined under the discipline of the monastery?

They rarely go abroad, they live in abstraction from the world, they have the poorest fare and the coarsest clothing; they labor much, speak little, watch long, rise early, continue long in prayer, read frequently, and keep themselves in complete discipline.

Observe the Carthusians, the Cistercians, and the monks and nuns of various orders, how do they every night rise to sing psalms to the Lord!

And therefore it is shameful to think that you should be so slothful about so holy a work, when so great a multitude have already commenced to sing praises to God.

Oh, that we had nothing else to do but always with our whole heart and our mouth to praise our Lord God!

Oh, that you might never have need to eat, or drink, or sleep; but might always praise God, and give yourself to spiritual exercises only; you should then be much more happy than you are now, when for so many necessities you must serve the flesh.

Would to God that these necessities did not exist, but only the spiritual refreshments of the soul, which, alas, we taste too seldom!

When a man has come to this, then he seeks comfort from no creature, then does he begin perfectly to relish God, then he will be contented with whatever may befall him.

Then he will neither rejoice for much nor be sorrowful for little, but he will commit himself entirely and confidently to God, who will be to him all in all, to whom nothing perishes nor dies, but all things live to him and obey his every word without delay.

Remember always your end, and how the time which is lost never returns.

Without care and diligence you will never get virtue.

If you begin to grow cold, it will begin to go ill with you.

But if you give yourself to fervor, you will find much peace, and feel less labor, through the assistance of God's grace and the love of virtue.

The fervent and diligent man is prepared for all things.

It is harder work to resist vices and passions than to toil in bodily labors.

He who does not shun small faults falls little by little into greater.

You will always rejoice in the evening, if you spend the day profitably.

Be watchful over yourself, stir up yourself, admonish yourself, and whatever becomes of others, neglect not yourself.

The more violence you do to yourself, the more you will profit. Amen.

THE SECOND BOOK

Admonitions Tending to Things Internal

Of the Inward Life

HE Kingdom of God is within you," [1] says the Lord.

Turn yourself with your whole heart to the Lord, and forsake this wretched world; and your soul will find rest.

Learn to despise outward things and to give yourself to things within; and you will see the Kingdom of God coming within you.

For the Kingdom of God is peace and joy in the Holy Ghost, which is not given to the wicked.

Christ will come to you and will show you his consolation, if you prepare for him a worthy mansion within you.

All his glory and beauty is from within, and there is his delight.

He frequently visits the inner man; sweet discourse, pleasant solace, much peace, familiarity exceedingly wonderful.

Go to, faithful soul, make ready your heart for this Bridegroom, that he may vouchsafe to come to you and dwell in you.

For thus he says: "If any man love me, he will keep my Commandments; and my Father will love

1—Luke, XVII, 21.

55

him, and we will come to him and make our abode with him." [2]

Make therefore room for Christ, and deny entrance to all others.

When you have Christ, you are rich, and you have enough.

He will be your provider and faithful watchman in all things, so that it will not be necessary to trust in men.

For men soon change, and swiftly pass away, but Christ remains forever, and stands firmly by us till the end.

No great trust should be placed in a frail and mortal man, even when he is useful and dear to us; neither ought we to be grieved when sometimes he opposes and contradicts us.

Those who are on your side to-day, may be against you to-morrow; and they often turn around as the wind.

Put all your trust in God, and let him alone be your fear and your love.

He will answer for you, and will do what is best for you.

"Here you have no continuing city," [3] and wherever you may be, you are a stranger and pilgrim; neither will you have any rest, unless you are firmly united with Christ.

Why do you here gaze about, since this is not the place of your rest?

In heaven ought to be your home, and all earthly things are to be looked upon as a passing show.

They all pass away and you alike with them.

2—John, XIV, 23.
3—Hebrews, XIII, 14.

Beware you cleave not to them, lest you be caught and perish.

Let your thought be on the Highest, and your prayer be continually directed to Christ.

If you cannot contemplate high and heavenly things, rest yourself in the passion of Christ, and dwell willingly in his sacred wounds.

For if you devoutly flee to the wounds and precious marks of Jesus, you will feel great comfort in tribulation; neither will you care for the slights of men, and will easily bear the words of detraction.

Christ was also in the world, despised of men, and when in greatest need, forsaken by friends and acquaintances, in the midst of slander.

Christ was willing to suffer and be despised; and dare you complain of any man?

Christ had adversaries and backbiters, and do you wish all men as your friends and benefactors?

Whence will your patience get its crown if no adversity befall you?

If you wish to suffer nothing, how will you be the friend of Christ?

Suffer with Christ and for Christ, if you desire to reign with Christ.

If you had but once perfectly entered into the inner life of Jesus, and had tasted a little of his ardent love, then you would not be anxious about your own convenience or inconvenience, but would rather rejoice at slander, because the love of Jesus makes a man despise himself.

A lover of Jesus, and inwardly true, and free from inordinate affections, can freely turn himself to God, and lift himself above himself in spirit, and rest fruitfully.

He who judges things as they are, not as they are said or esteemed to be, is truly wise, and taught more by God than by men.

He who knows how to walk, and to set little value upon outward things, neither requires places nor expects times for the performing of religious exercises.

The inward man quickly recollects himself, because he never pours out himself wholly to outward things.

He is not hindered by labor, nor by occupation necessary for the time being; but as things turn out, so he accommodates himself to them.

He who is well disposed, and well ordered within himself, does not care for the strange and perverse behavior of men.

A man is hindered and distracted in proportion as he draws matters to himself.

If it were well with you, and if you were well purified, all things would work out for your good and advancement.

For this cause many things displease and disturb you, that you are not yet perfectly dead to yourself, nor separated from all earthly things.

Nothing so defiles and entangles the heart of man as the foul longing for creatures.

If you refuse to be comforted outwardly, you will be able to contemplate heavenly things and frequently to rejoice inwardly.

CHAPTER II
Of Humble
Submission

Do not ponder on who is for you or against you, but mind and take care that God be with you in every-thing you do.

Have a good conscience, and God will well defend you.

He whom God wishes to aid cannot be hurt by anybody's perverseness.

If you know to be silent and to suffer, you will without doubt see the help of the Lord.

He knows the time and manner of delivering you, and therefore you ought to resign yourself to him.

It is God's work to help and deliver from all confusion.

It is often very helpful in increasing our humility that others know and rebuke our faults.

When a man humbles himself for his failings, he easily pleases others, and quickly satisfies those who are angered against him.

God protects and delivers the humble; the humble he loves and comforts.

Unto the humble man he inclines himself; unto the humble he grants great grace, and after his abasement raises him to glory.

Unto the humble he reveals his secrets, and draws and invites him to himself.

The humble person, when he is reproached, is yet in sufficient peace, because he rests on God and not on the world.

Do not fancy that you have made any progress, unless you feel yourself inferior to all.

CHAPTER III
*Of the Good
Peaceful Man*

First keep yourself in peace, and then you will be able to pacify others.

A peaceful man does more good than a well learned.

A passionate man turns even good into evil, and easily believes evil.

A good peaceful man turns everything into good.

He who is really in peace is suspicious of no one.

But he who is discontented and restless is tossed with divers suspicions.

He is neither quiet himself, nor suffers others to be quiet.

He often says that which he ought not to say, and omits that which is more expedient for him to do.

He considers what others are bound to do, but neglects that which he himself is bound to do.

Therefore be zealous first over yourself, and then you may justly be zealous also over your neighbor.

You know well how to excuse and color your deeds, and the excuses of others you do not wish to accept.

It would be more just if you accused yourself and excused your brother.

If you wish to be endured, endure also another.

See how far you are still from true love and humility, which does not know to be angry or offended with anybody, except with itself.

It is no great matter to associate with the good and gentle, for this is naturally pleasing to all, and everybody gladly has peace, and likes those who agree with him.

But to be able to live peacefully with the hard and perverse, with the disorderly, or with such as oppose us, that is a great grace, and a most praiseworthy manly thing.

There are some who keep themselves in peace, and also are in peace with others.

And there are some who neither have peace themselves, nor allow others to be in peace.

They are troublesome to others, but always more troublesome to themselves.

And there are some who remain in peace, and seek to bring others to peace.

Nevertheless our whole peace in this miserable world consists more in humble sufferance than in not experiencing adversities.

He who knows best how to suffer will possess the most peace.

He is the conqueror of himself and lord of the world, the friend of Christ and the inheritor of heaven.

CHAPTER IV
Of a Pure Mind and Simple Intention

By two wings is a man lifted up from earthly things, namely, simplicity and purity.

Simplicity ought to be in the intention, purity in the affection.

Simplicity reaches toward God; purity apprehends and tastes him.

No good action will hinder you, if inwardly you are free from inordinate affection.

If you reach after and seek nothing but the will of God and the good of your neighbor, you will enjoy inward liberty.

If your heart were right, then every creature would be to you a mirror of life and a book of holy doctrine.

There is no creature so small and abject that it does not represent God's goodness.

If you were inwardly good and pure, then you

would see and hear all things well without impediment.

A pure heart penetrates heaven and hell.

Such as each one is inwardly, so he judges outwardly.

If there is joy in the world, surely a man of pure heart possesses it.

And if there is anywhere tribulation and anxiety, an evil conscience knows it best.

Just as iron put into the fire loses its rust, and becomes altogether glowing, so the man who wholly turns himself to God is freed from slothfulness and transformed into a new man.

When a man begins to grow lukewarm, then he is afraid of a little labor, and gladly accepts external consolation.

But when he begins to overcome himself perfectly and to walk manfully in the way of God, then he esteems those things lighter which before seemed so grievous to him.

CHAPTER V
Of Self-Esteem

We cannot trust ourselves too much, because we often lack grace and understanding.

There is little light in us, and that which we have, we quickly lose through negligence.

Often we do not notice how blind we are within.

Often we commit evil and excuse it worse.

We are sometimes moved with passion, and we consider it zeal.

We reprehend small things in others, and pass over greater matters in ourselves.

Quickly enough we feel and weigh what we suffer

at the hands of others, but we mind not what others suffer from us.

He who well and rightly considers his own works will find little cause to judge hardly of others.

The inward man places his own cares before all others.

And he who diligently attends to himself easily keeps silence concerning others.

You will never live the inner life and be devout, unless you are silent concerning other people's affairs, and look specially to yourself.

When you attend wholly to yourself and to God, you will be little moved with the things you see outside.

Where are you, when you are not present to yourself?

And when you have overrun all things, what have you profited, if you neglected yourself?

If you would have peace and true harmony, you must put all things aside, and look only upon yourself.

From this you will get much profit, if you keep yourself free from all temporal care.

You will greatly fall back, if you set value upon any earthly thing.

Let there be nothing great to you, nothing high, nothing pleasing, nothing acceptable, but only God himself or the things of God.

Consider every comfort vain which you receive from any creature.

A soul that loves God looks down upon all things that are below God.

God alone is everlasting and of infinite greatness, the soul's solace, and the true joy of the heart.

CHAPTER VI
*Of the Joy
of a Good
Conscience*

The glory of a good man is the testimony of a good conscience.

Have a good conscience, and you will ever have joy.

A good conscience can bear many things, and is very joyful in adversities.

An evil conscience is always fearful and unquiet.

You will rest sweetly, if your heart does not reprehend you.

Do not rejoice unless you have done well.

The wicked never have true happiness nor feel inward peace, because "there is no peace for the wicked," [4] says the Lord.

And if they should say, "We are in peace, no evil shall befall us, and who shall dare to harm us?" believe them not, for suddenly the wrath of God will arise, and will reduce their deeds to nothings, and their thoughts will perish.

To glory in tribulation is no hard thing for him who loves, for so to glory is to glory in the cross of the Lord.

That glory is short which is given and accepted of men.

The glory of the world always accompanies sorrow.

The glory of the good is in their conscience, and not in the mouth of men.

The gladness of the just is of God and in God, and their joy is of the truth.

He who desires true and eternal glory cares not for that which is temporal.

And he who seeks temporal glory or does not

4—Isaiah, XLVIII, 22; LVII, 21.

despise it from his soul is proved to have but little love for heavenly glory.

He enjoys great tranquillity of heart, who cares neither for the praises nor the dispraises of men.

He will easily be content and pacified, whose conscience is pure.

You are not any more holy because you are praised, nor any more vile because you are reproached.

You are what you are, and you cannot be made greater by words than what you are in the sight of God.

If you consider what you are within, you will not care what people say about you.

"Man looks on the outward appearance, but the Lord looks on the heart." [5]

Man considers the deeds, but God weighs the intention.

To be always doing well, and to put little value on himself, is the sign of a humble soul.

Not to look for comfort from any creature, is a sign of great purity and inward faith.

He who seeks no witness for himself from without shows that he has wholly committed himself to God.

"For not he that commendeth himself is approved," as Paul says, "but whom the Lord commendeth." [6]

To walk inwardly with God, and not to be kept by any outward affection, is the state of a spiritual man.

5—I Samuel, XVI, 7.
6—II Corinthians, X, 18.

CHAPTER VII
*Of Loving
Jesus above
All Things*

Blessed is he who understands what it is to love Jesus, and to despise himself for Jesus' sake.

He must give up what he loves for his beloved, for Jesus will be loved alone above all things.

The love of creatures is deceitful and inconstant; the love of Jesus is faithful and lasting.

He who cleaves to a creature will fall with that which is frail; he who embraces Jesus will stand firmly forever.

Love him and keep him for your friend, who, when all go away, will not forsake you, nor will suffer you to perish in the end.

You must some day be separated from all, whether you will or no.

Keep close to Jesus in life and death, and commit yourself to his trust, who, when all fail, can alone help you.

Your beloved is of such a nature that he will admit of no rival, but wants to have your heart alone, and sit as a king on his own throne.

If you knew how to free yourself well from all things, Jesus would gladly dwell with you.

You will find almost everything a loss, which you repose in men, outside of Jesus.

Trust not nor lean upon a reed blown by the wind, for all flesh is grass and all its glory will wither as the flower of the grass.[7]

You will be quickly deceived if you only look to the outward appearance of men.

For if in others you seek comfort and gain, you will more often feel loss.

7—Isaiah, XL, 6.

If you seek Jesus in all things, you will surely find Jesus.

But if you seek yourself, you will also find yourself, but to your own destruction.

For man is more harmful to himself, if he does not seek Jesus, than the whole world and all his adversaries.

CHAPTER VIII
Of Familiar Friendship with Jesus

When Jesus is present, all is well, and nothing seems difficult.

But when Jesus is not present, all is hard.

When Jesus does not speak within, our comfort is worthless.

But if Jesus speaks a single word, great comfort is felt.

Did not Mary Magdalene rise immediately from the place where she wept, when Martha said to her, "The Master is here and calls for you"? [8]

Happy the hour when Jesus calls you from tears to the joy of the spirit.

How dry and hard are you without Jesus!

How foolish and vain, if you desire anything outside of Jesus!

Is this not a greater loss than if you lost the whole world?

What can the world profit you without Jesus?

To be without Jesus is a grievous hell, and to be with Jesus, a sweet paradise.

If Jesus be with you, no enemy will be able to hurt you.

He who finds Jesus, finds a good treasure, yea, good above all good.

8—John, XI, 28.

And he who loses Jesus, loses very, very much, and more than the whole world.

Most poor is he who lives without Jesus, and most rich who is well with Jesus.

It is a great skill to know how to live with Jesus, and to know how to keep Jesus is great wisdom.

Be humble and peaceful, and Jesus will be with you.

Be devout and quiet, and Jesus will remain with you.

You can easily drive Jesus away and lose his favor, if you will turn to the outward things.

And if you have put him to flight and lost him, to whom will you flee, and whom will you seek for a friend?

Without a friend you cannot live well, and if Jesus were not above all your friend, you would be exceedingly sad and desolate.

Foolishly therefore you act, if you confide and rejoice in any other.

It is preferable to have the whole world against you than to have Jesus offended with you.

Among all therefore that are dear to you, let Jesus be especially beloved.

Let all be loved for Jesus' sake, but Jesus for himself.

Jesus Christ alone is to be specially loved, who alone is found good and faithful above all friends.

For him, and in him, let friends as well as enemies be dear unto you, and pray for them all that they all may know and love him.

Never desire to be specially praised or loved, because that belongs to God alone, who has none like unto himself.

Nor desire that any one set his heart on you, nor set your heart on the love of any, but let Jesus be in you and in every good man.

Be pure and free within, not entangled with the love of any creature.

You must bring a bare and clean heart to God, if you wish to be free to see how gracious the Lord is.

And truly, unless you are prevented and drawn by his grace, you will never attain to this end, to forsake and dismiss all, that you may be united to him alone.

For when the grace of God comes to a man, then he becomes able to do all things.

And when it departs, then he is poor and weak, and as it were given up to beatings.

In this case he should not be dejected nor despair, but rest on the will of God, and bear all things which come upon him for the glory of Jesus Christ; because after winter comes summer, after night comes day, and after the tempest a great calm.

CHAPTER IX
Of the Want of All Comfort

It is no hard matter to despise human comfort, when we have divine.

It is a great and very great thing to be able to do without both human and divine comfort, and for God's honor willingly to bear misery of heart, and to seek one's self in nothing, nor to look to his own merit.

What great matter is it, if you are cheerful and devout at the coming of grace?

This hour is wished for of all men.

Quite softly does he ride whom the grace of God carries.

And what marvel if he does not feel his burden, who is carried by the Almighty, and led by the greatest guide?

We gladly have something for our comfort, and a man with difficulty strips himself of self.

The holy martyr Laurence overcame the world together with his priest, because whatever seemed delightful in the world he despised; and for the love of Christ he patiently suffered God's chief priest Sixtus, whom he most dearly loved, to be even taken away from him.[9]

He therefore conquered the love of man by the love of the Creator, and he rather chose God's good pleasure than human comfort.

So also you must learn for the love of God to part with even a near and dear friend; nor take it hard when you have been deserted by a friend, knowing that we all must be parted from each other at last.

Mightily and long must a man strive within himself, before he can learn fully to master himself, and to direct his whole desire toward God.

When a man leans on himself, he easily inclines toward human comforts.

But a true lover of Christ and a diligent seeker after virtue does not fall back upon comforts, nor does he seek such sweetness of sense, but rather hard exercises, and to sustain severe labors for Christ.

When therefore spiritual comfort is given by God, accept it with thanksgiving; but know that it is the gift of God, not any merit of yours.

Be not puffed up, be not too joyful nor presumptuous, but rather be the more humble for that gift,

9—See Augustine, *Tractatus in Joannis Evangelio*, XXVII; Ambrose, *De Officiis Ministrorum*, Book I, Chap. XLI.

more wary too and fearful in all your actions, because that hour will pass away, and temptation will
follow.

When comfort is taken away, do not at once
despair, but with humility and patience wait for
the heavenly visitation, for God is able to give back
to you more ample consolation.

This is not new nor strange to those who have had
experience in the way of God, for with the great
saints and the ancient prophets there was often this
manner of change.

Wherefore one said when the grace of God was
present, "I said in my prosperity, I shall never be
moved." [10]

But when grace had departed, he goes on to say
what he felt within himself: "Thou didst turn thy
face from me, and I was troubled." [11]

Meanwhile he nevertheless does not by any means
despair, but more earnestly beseeches the Lord, and
says, "Unto thee, O Lord, will I cry, and I will pray
unto my God." [12]

And then he receives the fruit of his prayer, and
testifies that he was heard, saying, "The Lord heard
me and had mercy upon me, the Lord was my
helper." [13]

But wherein?

"Thou hast turned," he says, "my heaviness into
joy, thou hast girded me with gladness." [14]

If it was thus with the great saints, we infirm and
needy need not despair, if sometimes we are fervent

10—Psalms, XXX, 6.
11—Psalms, XXX, 7.
12—Verse 8.
13—Verse 10.
14—Verse 11.

and sometimes cold, for the Spirit comes and goes, according to the good pleasure of his own will.

Wherefore the blessed Job says, "Thou dost visit him in the morning, and suddenly thou dost prove him." [15]

Upon which then can I hope, and in which ought I to trust, save in the great mercy of God alone, and in the sole hope of heavenly grace?

For whether I have with me good men or devout brethren or faithful friends, whether sacred books or beautiful treatises, or sweet hymns and songs; all these aid but little and have but little savor when I am deserted by grace and left in mine own poverty.

There is no better remedy, then, than patience and denial of self according to the will of God.

I have never found any man so religious and devout, who did not feel at times a withdrawal of grace, or a decrease of zeal.

No saint was so filled with rapture and so enlightened, but that sooner or later he was not tempted.

For he is not worthy of the high contemplation of God, who for God's sake has not experienced some tribulation.

For temptation is wont to go before as a sign of comfort to follow.

For unto those who are proved by temptations, heavenly comfort is promised.

He says, "He that shall overcome, I will give him to eat of the tree of life." [16]

But divine consolation is given, in order that man become stronger to bear adversities.

15—Job, VII, 18.
16—Revelation, II, 7.

Then follows also temptation, lest he should lift up himself because of the benefit.

The devil sleeps not, nor is the flesh as yet dead; therefore do not cease to prepare yourself for the battle, for on your right hand and on your left are enemies who never rest.

CHAPTER X
*Of Gratitude
for the Grace
of God*

Why do you seek rest, since you were born to labor?

Dispose yourself to patience rather than to comfort, and to the bearing of the cross rather than to gladness.

Who among the men in the world would not gladly accept comfort and spiritual joy, if he could always have it?

For spiritual comforts exceed all the delights of the world and pleasures of the flesh.

For all the delights of the world are either vain or unclean.

Spiritual delights, however, are only pleasant and honest, sprung from virtue, and infused by God into pure minds.

But no one can always enjoy these divine comforts according to his desire, because the time of temptation does not cease for long.

Great is the difference between a visitation from above, and false liberty of mind and great confidence in one's self.

God does well in giving the grace of comfort, but man does ill in not returning all to God with thanksgiving.

And therefore the gifts of grace cannot flow in us, because we are ungrateful to the author of them, nor do we return all to the original fountain.

For grace always attends him who is duly thankful, and from the proud shall be taken what is wont to be given to the humble.[17]

I desire no consolation which takes from me compunction.

Nor do I affect that contemplation which leads to haughtiness of mind.

For all that is high is not holy, nor all that is sweet, good; every desire is not pure, nor everything that is dear to us, pleasing to God.

I gladly accept that grace whereby I am ever made more humble and timid, more ready to renounce myself.

He who is made learned by the gift of grace, and taught by the stroke of its withdrawal, does not dare to attribute any good to himself, but rather will acknowledge himself poor and naked.

"Give unto God that which is of God," [18] and ascribe to yourself what is your own; that is, give thanks to God for his grace, but to yourself give the blame, and note that your punishment is deserved for your fault.

Put yourself always in the lowest place, and the highest shall be given to you, for the highest cannot stand without the lowest.

The greatest saints before God are the least in their own judgment.

The more glorious they are, the more humble within themselves.

Those who are filled with truth and heavenly glory are not desirous of boasting.

17—See introduction, p. xxviii.
18—Matthew, XXII, 21.

Those who are firmly settled and grounded in God can in no way be proud.

And those who ascribe all unto God, whatsoever good they have received, do not seek glory of each other, but wish for the glory which comes from God alone, and desire that God be praised above all things in themselves and in all the saints; and they are always tending to this very thing.

Be therefore thankful for the least, and you will be worthy to receive the greater.

Let the smallest be to you as the greatest, and that which is of less account as a special gift.

If you regard the dignity of the giver, no gift will seem small or very cheap.

For that is not small which is given by the Most High God.

Even if he should give punishment and stripes, it ought to be welcome, because he does it always for our welfare, whatever he permits to happen to us.

He who desires to keep the grace of God, let him be thankful for the grace given, and patient when it is taken away.

Let him pray that it may return; let him be cautious and humble, lest he lose it.

CHAPTER XI
Of the Small Number of Those Who Love the Cross of Jesus

Jesus has now many lovers of his heavenly kingdom, but few bearers of his cross.

He has many desirous of comfort, but few of tribulation.

He finds many companions of his table, but few of his abstinence.

All desire to rejoice with him; few are willing to undergo anything for his sake.

Many follow Jesus unto the breaking of the bread, but few unto the drinking of the cup of his passion.

Many reverence his miracles; few follow the ignominy of the cross.

Many love Jesus so long as no adversities befall them.

Many praise and bless him, so long as they receive any comforts from him.

But if Jesus hide himself and leave them but a little while, they fall either into complaining or into too much dejection of mind.

Those who love Jesus for Jesus' sake, and not for some comfort of their own, bless him in all tribulation and anguish of heart as well as in the greatest comfort.

And if he should never wish to give them comfort, they nevertheless praise [19] him always, and always are willing to render thanks.

Oh, how powerful is the pure love of Jesus which is mixed with no selfishness!

Are not all those to be called mercenary, who are ever seeking comforts?

Do they not prove themselves lovers of self more than of Christ, who are always thinking of their own profit and advantage?

Where shall he be found who is willing to serve God for nothing?

Rarely is any one found so spiritual as to be stripped of everything.

For who shall find one truly poor in spirit, and free of all created things?

19—Hagen has "love."

From afar, yea, from the ends of the earth, is his value.

If a man gave all his substance, yet it is nothing; and if he practised great repentance, still it is little; and if he understood all knowledge, he is still afar off; and if he had great virtue, and very ardent devotion, he still lacks much, namely, this one thing which is most necessary to him.

What is that?

That leaving all, he forsake himself, and go wholly forth from himself, and retain nothing of selfishness.

And when he has done all that he knows must be done, let him think he has done nothing; let him not reckon that much which might be much esteemed, but let him pronounce himself to be in truth an unprofitable servant; as the Truth says, "When ye have done all things that are commanded you, say, We are unprofitable servants." [20]

Then may he be truly poor and naked in spirit, and say with the prophet, "For I am alone and poor." [21]

Nevertheless no man is richer than he, no man more powerful, no man more free; for he knows both how to give up himself and all things, and to set himself in the lowest place.

CHAPTER XII
*Of the Royal
Way of the
Holy Cross*

This seems to many a hard saying: "Deny thyself, take up thy cross, and follow Jesus." [22]

But much harder will it be to hear that last word: "Depart from me, ye cursed, into the everlasting fire." [23]

20—Luke, XVII, 10.
21—Psalms, XXV, 16.
22—Matthew, XVI, 24.
23—Matthew, XXV, 41.

For they who now gladly hear and follow the word of the cross, will not then fear the sentence of eternal damnation.

This sign of the cross will be in heaven, when the Lord will come to judgment.

Then all the servants of the cross, who in their lifetime conformed themselves unto the Crucified, will draw near unto Christ the Judge with great confidence.

Why then do you fear to take up the cross which leads to heaven?

In the cross is salvation, in the cross is life; in the cross is protection from enemies, in the cross is infusion of heavenly sweetness; in the cross is strength of mind; in the cross joy of spirit, in the cross the height of virtue, in the cross the perfection of sanctity.

There is no salvation of the soul, nor hope of everlasting life, but in the cross.

Take up therefore your cross and follow Jesus, and you will go into the life everlasting.

He went before, bearing his cross, and died for you on the cross; and you may also bear your cross and desire to die on the cross.

For if you be dead with him, you will also live with him.

And if you be a companion in punishment, you will also be one in glory.

Behold! in the cross all does consist, and on dying all depends; and there is no other way to life and to true inward peace, but by the way of the Holy Cross and daily mortification.

Go where you will, seek what you will, you shall

not find a higher way above, nor a safer way below, than the way of the Holy Cross.

Dispose and order all things according to your will and judgment, and you will ever find something that you must suffer, either willingly or against your will; and so you will ever find the cross.

You will either feel pain in the body, or you will suffer in the soul the tribulation of spirit.

Sometimes you will be forsaken of God, sometimes you will be troubled by your neighbor; and what is more, oftentimes you will be wearisome to yourself; neither can you be delivered or eased by any remedy or solace, but so long as it pleases God you ought to bear it.

For God wills that you learn to suffer tribulation without comfort, and that you subject yourself wholly to him, and be made more humble by the tribulation.

No one feels the passion of Christ with his heart as he who has suffered the like himself.

The cross is therefore always ready, and everywhere is waiting for you.

You cannot flee from it, wherever you may run, because wherever you go you carry yourself with you, and you will always find yourself.

Turn yourself above, turn yourself below, turn yourself without, turn yourself within, and in all these places you will find the cross; and it is necessary that everywhere you have patience, if you wish to have inward peace and earn an everlasting crown.

If you bear the cross gladly, it will carry you and lead you to the desired end, where there shall be no more suffering, although here that shall not be.

If you bear it unwillingly, you make a burden for yourself, and load yourself the more, and nevertheless you must needs suffer.

If you cast away one cross, you will without doubt find another one, and perhaps a heavier one.

Do you believe to escape that which no mortal being can avoid?

Which of the saints in the world was without cross and tribulation?

For not even Jesus Christ our Lord was ever one hour without the anguish of his passion.

"Christ," says he, "must needs suffer, and rise again from the dead, and so enter into his glory." [24]

And how do you seek any other way than this royal way which is the way of the Holy Cross?

The whole life of Christ was a cross and a martyrdom, and you seek rest and joy?

You err, you err, if you seek any other thing than to suffer tribulations, because this whole mortal life is full of miseries, and signed on every side with crosses.

And the higher a person has advanced in spirit, the heavier he often finds the crosses, because the punishment of his exile increases with his love.

Nevertheless this man, who is in so many ways afflicted, is not without the refreshment of consolation, because he feels that very much benefit accrues to him by the enduring of his cross.

For while he willingly submits himself to it, every burden of tribulation is turned into an assurance of divine consolation.

And the more the flesh is wasted by affliction, the more is the spirit strengthened by inward grace.

24—Luke, XXIV, 46.

At times he is so comforted by the suffering of tribulation and adversity, for the love of conforming to the cross of Christ, that he does not want to be without grief and tribulation; because he believes that he will be the more acceptable unto God, the more and the heavier burdens he can bear for him.

This is not the virtue of man, but the grace of Christ, which can and does so much in the weak flesh, that what it naturally always hates and flees from, by fervor of spirit, it encounters and loves.

It is not in the nature of man to bear the cross, to love the cross, to chastise the body and subject it to servitude, to flee honors, gladly to suffer reproaches, to despise one's self and to wish to be despised, to endure all adversities and losses, and to desire no prosperity in the world.

If you look to yourself, you will be able of yourself to do nothing of this kind.

But if you trust in the Lord, strength will be given to you from heaven, and the world and the flesh will be made subject to your command.

Neither will you fear your enemy the devil, if you are armed with faith and signed with the cross of Christ.

Set yourself, therefore, like a good and faithful servant of Christ, to bear manfully the cross of your Lord, who out of love was crucified for you.

Prepare yourself to bear many adversities and various kinds of troubles in this miserable life, because so it will be with you wherever you are, and so you will surely find it, wherever you hide yourself.

So it must be, nor is there any means to escape from tribulation and sorrow but only to endure yourself.

Drink affectionately of the Lord's cup, if you desire to be his friend and to have part with him.

Leave consolations to God; let him do therein as shall best please him.

But do you set yourself to suffer tribulations, and reckon them the greatest comforts, for the sufferings of the present time are not worthy to earn the future glory,[25] even though you alone could bear them all.

When you shall come to this, that tribulation will seem sweet, and you will relish it for Christ's sake; then think it is well with you, for you have found paradise on earth.

As long as it is hard for you to suffer, and you desire to flee from it, so long will you be ill at ease, and the desire of escaping tribulation will follow you everywhere.

If you set yourself to that which you ought to do, namely, to suffer and to die, it will quickly be better with you, and you will find peace.

Even though you were caught up into the third heaven with Paul, you will not on that account be secure from evil.

"I will show him," says Jesus, "how much he ought to suffer for my name's sake." [26]

Suffering then will stay by you, if it please you to love Jesus and to serve him perpetually.

Oh, that you were worthy to suffer something for the name of Jesus; how great a glory would remain unto you, what joy would come to all the saints of God, what edification also to your neighbor!

For all men commend patience, although few are willing to suffer.

25—Romans, VIII, 14.
26—Acts, IX, 16.

You surely ought gladly to suffer a little for Christ, since many suffer more grievous things for the world.

Know for certain that you ought to lead a dying life.

And the more a person dies to himself, the more he begins to live unto God.

No one is fit to comprehend heavenly things, unless he submit himself to the bearing of adversities for Christ.

Nothing is more acceptable to God, nothing more wholesome to you in this world, than to suffer gladly for Christ.

And if you could choose, you ought rather to wish to suffer adversities for Christ, than to be refreshed with many consolations, because you will be more like Christ, and conformed to all the saints.

For our worthiness and growth in grace does not consist in many delights and consolations, but rather in bearing great afflictions and tribulations.

Indeed if there had been anything better and more profitable to the salvation of man than suffering, surely Christ would have shown it by word and example.

For both the disciples who followed him, and also all who desired to follow him, he plainly exhorts to the bearing of the cross, and says, "If any one will come after me, let him deny himself, and take up his cross, and follow me." [27]

So that when we have thoroughly read and searched all, let this be the final conclusion: "That through many tribulations we must enter into the kingdom of God." [28]

27—Matthew, XVI, 24.
28—Acts, XIV, 22.

THE THIRD BOOK

OF INWARD CONSOLATION

Of the Inward Speech of Christ to the Faithful Soul

I WILL harken what the Lord God will say within me.[1]

Blessed is the soul which hears the Lord speaking within it, and from his mouth receives the word of consolation.

Blessed are the ears which catch the throbbing whisper of the Lord, and give no heed to the many whisperings of this world.

Blessed truly are those ears which listen not to the voice sounding without, but to the Truth teaching inwardly.

Blessed are the eyes which are closed to outward things, but intent on inward things.

Blessed are they who search inward things and study to prepare themselves more and more, by daily exercises, for the receiving of heavenly mysteries.

Blessed are they who long to devote their time to God, and shake off all worldly impediments.

Consider this, O my soul, and close the gates of your sensual desires, that you may hear what the Lord God will say within you.

1—Psalms, LXXXV. 8.

This says the beloved: I am your Salvation, your Peace, and your Life.

Keep yourself near me, and you will find peace.

Let all transitory things go, and seek the eternal.

What are all temporal things but seducing snares?

And what avail all the created things, if you are forsaken by the Creator?

Put therefore all things away, and give yourself to your Creator, to be pleasing and faithful to him, that you may be able to attain true blessedness.

CHAPTER II
That the Truth Teaches Inwardly without Noise of Words

Speak, O Lord, for thy servant heareth.[2]

I am thy servant; give me understanding, that I may know thy testimonies.[3]

Incline my heart to the words of thy mouth; let thy speech distil as the dew.

The children of Israel spoke in olden days to Moses: "Speak thou unto us, and we will hear; let not the Lord speak unto us, lest we die."[4]

Not so, Lord, not so, I beseech thee; but rather with the prophet Samuel, I humbly and earnestly entreat, "Speak, Lord, for thy servant heareth."

Let not Moses speak unto me, nor any of the prophets, but rather do thou speak, O Lord God, who didst inspire and illuminate all the prophets; for thou alone without them canst perfectly instruct me, but they without thee profit nothing.

They can indeed sound forth words, but they do not give spirit.

2—I Samuel, III, 9.
3—Psalms, CXIX, 125.
4—Exodus, XX, 19.

They speak beautifully, but when thou art silent they do not inflame the heart.

They hand books to us, but thou openest the senses.

They bring mysteries, but thou unlockest the meaning of sealed things.

They declare commandments, but thou helpest to fulfil them.

They show the way, but thou givest strength to walk in it.

They act only outwardly, but thou instructest and enlightenest the heart.

They water outwardly, but thou givest fruitfulness.

They cry with words, but thou impartest understanding to the hearing.

Let not Moses therefore speak unto me, but thou, O Lord, my God, the Everlasting Truth, lest I die and prove unfruitful, if I be only warmed outwardly, and not inflamed within; lest it turn to my condemnation—the word heard but not followed, known but not loved, believed but not observed.

Speak, therefore, Lord; thy servant heareth; for thou hast the words of eternal life.

Speak unto me for some consolation of my soul, for the amendment of my whole life, but to thy praise and glory and eternal honor.

CHAPTER III
That the Words of God Are to be Heard with Humility and That Many Heed Them Not

"Hear, my son, my words, the sweetest words, surpassing all the knowledge of the philosophers and wise men of this world.

"My words are spirit and life,[5] and are not to be weighed by the understanding of man.

"They are not to be drawn forth for vain approbation, but to be heard in silence, and to be received with all humility and great affection."

And I said: "Blessed is the man whom thou teachest, O Lord, and instructest him in thy Law.

"That thou mayest give him rest from the evil days,[6] and that he be not desolate on the earth."

"I," saith the Lord, "taught the prophets from the beginning, and even to this day I cease not to speak to all; but many are hardened, and deaf to my voice.

"Most people rather listen to the world than to God; they sooner follow the desires of their own flesh than God's good pleasure.

"The world promises things temporal and mean, and is served with great eagerness; I promise things most high and eternal, and the hearts of mortals remain unreceptive.

"Who serves and obeys me with such great care as the world and its lords are served?

"Be ashamed, O Sidon, saith the sea.[7]

"And if you wish to know the cause, hear wherefore.

"For a small reward a long journey is undertaken;

5—John, VI, 63.
6—Psalms, XCIV, 13.
7—Isaiah, XXIII, 4.

for the life eternal many will scarcely lift a foot once from the ground.

"Mean reward is sought after; for a single piece of money sometimes there is shameful contention; for a vain thing and a trifling promise men shrink not from toiling day and night. But, alas! for an unchangeable good, for an inestimable reward, for the highest honor, and glory without end, they grudge even the least fatigue.

"Be ashamed, therefore, thou slothful and discontented servant, that they are found more ready to destruction than thou to life.

"They rejoice more in vanity than thou dost in the truth.

"Sometimes indeed they are frustrated of their hope, but my promise deceiveth none, nor sendeth him away that trusteth in me.

"What I have promised, I will give; what I have said, I will fulfil; if only some one remain faithful in my love even to the end.

"I am the rewarder of all good men, and the strong approver of all the devout.

"Write my words in thy heart and consider them diligently, for in time of temptation they will be very needful to thee.

"What thou understandest not when thou readest, thou shalt know in the day of visitation.

"In two ways I am wont to visit mine elect, namely, with temptation and with consolation.

"And I daily read two lessons to them, one in reproving their vices, another in exhorting them to virtues.

"He who hath my words and despiseth them, hath one who shall judge him in the last day."

CHAPTER IV [8]
*A Prayer
for the Grace
of Devotion*

O Lord my God! Thou art all my good.

And who am I that I should dare to speak to thee?

I am thy poorest servant, an abject worm, much more poor and contemptible than I can or dare express.

Yet do thou remember, O Lord, that I am nothing, I have nothing, and I can do nothing.

Thou alone art good, just, and holy; thou canst do all things, thou accomplishest all things, thou fillest all things, only the sinner thou leavest empty.

Remember thy mercies, and fill my heart with thy grace; thou wilt not that thy words should be void and vain.

How can I endure this miserable life, unless thou strengthen me with thy mercy and grace?

Turn not thy face away from me; delay not thy visitation; withdraw not thy consolation; lest my soul become unto thee as a thirsty land without water.

Teach me, O Lord, to do thy will; teach me to live worthily and humbly in thy sight, for thou art my wisdom, who knowest me in truth, and didst know me before the world was made, and before I was born in the world.

CHAPTER V
*That One Ought
to Live in Truth
and Humility
before God*

"My son.

"Walk before me in truth, and ever seek me in the simplicity of thy heart.

"He who walketh before me in truth, shall be defended from evil assaults, and the truth shall

8—This is not a separate chapter in the edition of Thomas a Kempis.

deliver him from the wiles and slanders of wicked men.

"If the truth make thee free, thou shalt be free indeed, and shalt not care for the vain words of men.[9]

"Reflect on thy sins with great displeasure and sorrow, and never think thyself anything because of any good works.

"Verily thou art a sinner; thou art subject to many passions and entangled in them.

"Of thyself thou always tendest to nothing; thou quickly stumblest, art quickly overcome, quickly disordered, quickly dissolved.

"Thou hast nothing whereof thou canst glory, but many things for which thou shouldst reckon thyself vile; for thou art much weaker than thou art able to comprehend.

"Let therefore nothing seem great to thee, whatsoever thou doest.

"Let nothing seem important, nothing precious and wonderful, nothing worthy of esteem, nothing lofty, nothing praiseworthy and desirable, but that alone which is eternal.

"Let the eternal truth please thee above all things; let thy own extreme unworthiness be always displeasing to thee.

"Fear nothing, blame nothing, flee nothing so much as thy faults and sins, which ought to be more displeasing to thee than any losses whatever of goods.

"Some walk not sincerely before me, but being led by a certain curiosity and pride, wish to know my secrets, and to understand the deep things of

9—Thomas a Kempis adds one of his characteristic interruptions.

God, while they neglect themselves and their salvation.

"These often fall into great temptations and sins because of their pride and curiosity, since I am against them.

"Fear the judgments of God, and dread the wrath of the Omnipotent.

"Do not discuss the works of the Most High, but search diligently thine own iniquities, in what great sins thou hast fallen, and how many good things thou hast neglected.

"Some carry their devotion only in books, some in pictures, some in outward signs and figures.

"Some have me in their mouths, but little in their hearts.

"Others there are who, being illuminated in their understanding and purged in their affections, continually long after things eternal, hear unwillingly of earthly things, and serve with grief the necessities of nature; and these feel that the spirit of truth is speaking within them, because it teacheth them to despise earthly things and to love heavenly things, to neglect the world, and to long for heaven all the day and night."

CHAPTER VI
Of the
Wonderful
Effect of
Divine Love[10]

Love is a great thing, an exceedingly great good, which alone makes light everything that is heavy; and it makes equal all that is unequal.

For it carries a burden without feeling it, and makes sweet and tasteful everything that is bitter.

The noble love of Jesus impels one to do great

10—Thomas a Kempis adds a prayer.

things, and incites him to be always longing for what is more perfect.

Love desires to be lifted up, and will not be held down by things below.

Love wants to be free, and aloof from all worldly affections, lest its inward sight be hindered, lest it be entangled by any temporal prosperity, or overcome by adversity.

Nothing is sweeter than love, nothing stronger, nothing loftier, nothing wider, nothing pleasanter, nothing fuller or better in heaven and on earth; because love is born of God, and cannot rest but in God, above all created things.

Love [11] flies, runs, and rejoices; it is free and not hindered.

It does not respect the gifts, but turns itself above all goods to the Giver.

Love often knows no measure, but is fervent beyond all measure.

Love feels no burden, thinks nothing of labor, attempts more than it is able to do, pleads not impossibility, because it thinks that it can do all things. [12]

Love is watchful, and sleeping does not slumber; when weary, it is not tired, when frightened, not confused, but as a living flame and burning torch, it forces itself upward, and goes securely on its way. [13]

Love is swift, sincere, pious, pleasant, and lovely; strong, patient, faithful, prudent, long-suffering, manly, and never seeking itself.

11—Thomas a Kempis changes the subject into "he who loves" and adds one sentence.

12—Thomas a Kempis adds one sentence.

13—Thomas a Kempis adds seven sentences, again changing the subject.

For when one seeks himself, there he falls from love.

Love is circumspect, humble, and upright; not weak, not fickle, nor intent on vain things; moderate, chaste, steadfast.[14]

He who is not ready to suffer all things, and to conform to the will of his beloved, is not worthy to be called a lover.

A lover ought to embrace gladly all that is hard and bitter for the sake of the beloved, and not be drawn away from him for any contrary accidents.

CHAPTER VII
Of the Proof of
the True Lover

"My son, thou art not yet a courageous and considerate lover." Wherefore, Lord?

"Because for a slight opposition thou leavest off where thou hast begun, and too eagerly seekest consolation.

"A courageous lover standeth firm in temptations, and doth not believe the crafty persuasions of the enemy.

"As I please him in prosperity, so in adversity I do not displease him.

"A prudent lover regardeth not so much the gift of the lover, as the love of the giver.

"He esteemeth the affection more than the value, and setteth all gifts below the beloved.

"A noble lover resteth not in the gift, but in me above every gift.

"Hence all is not lost if sometimes thou think less of me and of my saints than thou wouldst.

14—Thomas a Kempis adds one sentence and a few words to the preceding.

"That good and sweet affection, which thou some-times perceivest, is the effect of present grace, and a foretaste of the heavenly country.

"But hereon thou must not lean too much, for it goeth and cometh.

"But to strive against the evil motions arising in the mind, and to scorn the suggestions of the devil, is a token of virtue and of great merit.

"Let not therefore strange fancies trouble thee, no matter on what subject they crowd into thy mind.

"Firmly keep thy purpose, and an upright inten-tion toward God.

"Neither is it an illusion when sometimes thou suddenly lettest thyself be carried away to a change.[15]

"For these fancies thou dost rather unwillingly suffer than that thou committest them; and so long as they displease thee, and thou strivest against them, it is merit and not loss.

"Know that the enemy by all means doth strive to hinder thy longing after good, and to deter thee from every devout exercise; namely, from the rever-ence for the saints and the commemoration of my passion, from the profitable remembrance of sins, from the guard of thine own heart, and from the firm purpose of advancing in virtue.

"Many evil thoughts doth he suggest to thee, that he may work weariness and horror within thee, to draw thee away from prayer and holy reading.

"Humble confession is displeasing to him, and if he could, he would make thee cease from communion.

"Do not believe him, nor heed him, although he should often lay for thee snares of deceit.

15—Thomas a Kempis has a longer sentence.

"Blame him, when he suggesteth evil and unclean thoughts.

"Say to him, 'Go away, thou unclean spirit! be ashamed, thou wretch! thou art most unclean to bring such things to my ears.

" 'Depart from me, thou wicked seducer! thou shalt have no part in me; but Jesus shall be with me as a brave warrior, and thou shalt stand confounded.

" 'I would rather die and suffer any torment than consent to thee.

" 'Hold thy peace and be silent; I will hear thee no more, though thou shouldst cause me still more trouble.

" 'The Lord is my Light and my Salvation; whom shall I fear?

" 'Though a host of men should rise up against me, yet shall not my heart be afraid.

" 'The Lord is my Strength and my Redeemer.' [16]

"Fight as a good soldier, and if thou sometimes fail through weakness, put on more strength than before, trusting in my abundant grace, and take great heed of vain self-complacency and of pride.

"Through this many are led into error, and sometimes fall into blindness almost incurable.

"Let the fall of the proud, who foolishly lift up themselves, be to thee a warning and a source of constant humility."

16—Psalms, XXVII, 1-3; XIX, 14.

CHAPTER VIII
*Of Concealing
Grace under
the Guard of
Humility*

"My son.

"It is better and safer for thee to conceal the grace of devotion, and not to lift thyself up on high, nor to speak much thereof, nor to value it greatly, but rather to despise thyself, and to fear that it might have been given to one unworthy of it.

"One should not depend too much upon this feeling, for it can very quickly be turned into its opposite.

"Think, when thou art in a state of grace, how miserable and needy thou art wont to be without grace.

"Nor is it in this only that thy progress in spiritual life consisteth, when thou hast the grace of consolation; but rather when with humility, self-denial, and patience thou endurest the withdrawing thereof; so that thou relax not in the exercise of prayer, nor neglect the other duties thou art wont to perform; rather do thou to the best of thy ability and understanding perform gladly what lieth in thee, and do not wholly neglect thyself because of the dryness and anxiety of mind which thou feelest.

"For there are many who, when they do not succeed as they desire, become forthwith impatient or slothful.

"For the way of a man is not always in his power, but it belongeth to God to give, and to comfort, when he will, and how much he will, and whom he will; as it shall please him, and no more.

"Some, who were imprudent because of the grace of devotion within them, have destroyed themselves; because they attempted more than they were able to perform, not weighing the measure of their own weakness; but followed more the desire of their heart than the judgment of their reason.

"And because they presumed beyond what was pleasing to God, they therefore quickly lost his grace.

"They who had built themselves nests in heaven have become poor and have been left vile, so that, being humbled and impoverished, they might learn not to fly with their own wings, but to trust under my feathers.

"They who are as yet novices and inexperienced in the way of the Lord, unless they govern themselves after the counsel of the wise, may easily be deceived and broken to pieces.

"And if they will rather follow their own notions than believe others who are more experienced, their end will be dangerous, at least if they are unwilling to be drawn away from their own notion.

"Those who think themselves wise seldom let themselves be led patiently by others.

"It is better to have a small portion of good sense with humility, and a slender understanding, than great treasures of knowledge with vain self-complacency.

"It is better for thee to have less than to have much, of which thou mightest be proud.

"He doth not act discreetly enough who giveth himself wholly to joy, forgetting his former poverty and the chaste fear of the Lord, which is afraid of losing the grace which hath been offered.

"Nor hath he enough knowledge of virtue who in time of adversity and any trouble beareth himself too despairingly, and thinketh less confidingly of me than he ought.

"He who in time of peace is willing to be too secure shall be often found in time of war too much dejected and full of fears.

"If thou knewest always how to continue humble and moderate within thyself, and also to guide and rule thy spirit well, thou wouldst not so quickly fall into danger and offense.

"It is good counsel, that when fervor of spirit is kindled within thee, thou shouldst consider how it will be, when that light shall leave thee.

"And when this doth happen, then remember that the light may return again, which, as a warning to thyself and for mine own glory, I have withdrawn for a time.

"Such a trial is often more profitable than if thou shouldst always have things prosper according to thy will.

"For merits are not to be esteemed by the number of visions and comforts a man hath, nor by his skill in the Scriptures, nor by his being placed in a high station; but by this, that he be grounded in true humility, and be full of divine charity, that he always purely and uprightly seeketh the honor of God, that he thinketh nothing of and unfeignedly despiseth himself, and even rejoiceth more to be despised and humbled by others than to be honored."

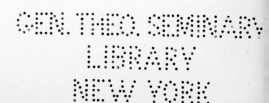

CHAPTER IX [17]
That All Things Are to Be Referred to God, as the Final End

"My son.

"I must be thy supreme and ultimate end, if thou desire to be truly blessed.

"Through this intention thy affection will be purified, which is too often sinfully bent on itself and on creatures.

"For when thou seekest thyself in anything, immediately thou faintest and growest barren.

"Therefore refer everything to me, because it is I who have given thee all.

"Look upon each thing as flowing from the Highest Good, and therefore everything should be attributed to me as to its source.

"From me, as from a living fountain, the small and the great, the poor and the rich, do draw the water of life; and they who willingly and gladly serve me will receive grace for grace.

"But he who will glory apart from me, or will take pleasure in some particular good, shall not stand firmly and securely in true joy, and shall not be enlarged in his heart, but frequently shall be hindered and straitened.

"Thou oughtst therefore to ascribe nothing of good to thyself, nor do thou attribute goodness to any man, but give everything to God, without whom man hath nothing.

"I gave all, I will receive all again, and with great strictness do I require a return of thanks.

"This is the truth by which vainglory is put to flight.

"And if the heavenly grace and the true love enter

17—Thomas a Kempis inserts one chapter.

in, there shall be no envy nor straitening of the heart, nor shall any selfish love predominate.

"For divine love overcometh all things, and enlargeth all the powers of the soul.

"If thou judge rightly, thou wilt rejoice in me alone, hope in me alone; because no one is good save God alone." [18]

CHAPTER X [19]
That the Desires of the Heart Are to Be Examined and Moderated

"My son.

"Thou hast still many things to learn, which thou hast not well learned yet."

What are they, Lord?

"That thou place thy desires wholly in subjection to my good pleasure, and that thou be not a lover of thyself, but an earnest follower of my will.

"Desires often inflame thee, and drive thee forward with vehemence; but consider whether thou be moved more for my honor than for thine own advantage.

"If I am the cause, then thou wilt be well content with whatsoever I shall ordain.

"But if there lurk in it any self-seeking, behold this it is that hindereth thee and weigheth thee down.

"Beware, therefore, that thou incline not too much to a desire formed before asking my counsel, lest perhaps afterward thou repent of it, or thou be displeased with that which at first pleased thee, and for which thou didst long as a greater good.

"For not every affection which seemeth good is

18—Luke, XVIII, 19.

19—Thomas a Kempis adds another chapter, interrupting the Lord by saying, "Now will I speak again, O Lord."

immediately to be followed, nor again is every opposite affection at the first to be avoided.

"It is sometimes expedient to use a little restraint
even in good endeavors and desires, lest through
importunity thou incur distraction of mind, lest
through want of discipline thou become a stumbling-
block to others, or lest by the resistance of others
thou art suddenly disturbed and so fall.

"Sometimes, however, thou must use violence and
resist manfully the sensual appetite, and not regard
what the flesh would or would not; but rather
take pains that it even against its will be made subject to the spirit.

"And so long ought it to be chastised and be
forced to remain subject to servitude, until it be
prepared for everything, and learn to be content
with a little, and be pleased with plain and simple
things, nor murmur against any inconvenience."

CHAPTER XI
*Of the Growth
of Patience and
the Struggle
against Evil
Desires*

O Lord God, I see that patience is
necessary for me, for many things in
this life fall out contrary.

For whatever plans I shall devise
for my own peace, my life cannot be
without strife and affliction.

"It is so, my son.

"But my will is that thou seek not that peace
which is without temptations, or which knoweth
nothing contrary; but rather think that thou hast
then found peace, when thou art tormented by temptations and tried in many adversities.

"If thou say that thou art not able to suffer much,
how then wilt thou endure the purging fire hereafter?

"Of two evils the lesser is always to be chosen.

"That thou mayest escape future punishments,[20] endeavor to endure present evils patiently for God's sake.

"Or dost thou believe that the men of this world suffer nothing, or but a little?

"Thou shalt find it otherwise, even though thou find out those who are most favored.

"But thou wilt say that they have many delights, and follow their own wills, and thus they think little of their afflictions.

"Be it so, that they do have whatever they will.

"But how long thinkest thou that it will last?

"Behold, the wealthy of this world shall be consumed as smoke, and there shall be no memory of their past joys!

"Yea, even while they are yet alive, they do not rest in them without bitterness and weariness and fear.

"For from the very same thing wherein they find delight, they often receive the penalty of sorrow.

"And justly so, that as they inordinately seek pleasures, and follow them, they enjoy them not without shame and bitterness.

"Oh, how brief, how false, how inordinate and filthy, are all these pleasures!

"Yet so drunken and blind are men that they understand it not; but like dumb beasts, for the sake of a little pleasure of this corruptible life, they incur death of the soul.

"Thou therefore, my son, go not after thy lusts, but refrain thyself from thine appetites.

20—Thomas a Kempis has "eternal torments."

"Delight thou in the Lord, and he shall give thee thy heart's desire.[21]

"For if thou wilt have true delight, and be more plentifully comforted by me; behold, in the contempt of all worldly things, and in the cutting off of all base delights, shall be thy blessing, and abundant consolation shall be given thee.

"And the more thou withdrawest thyself from all solace of creatures, the more sweet and powerful consolations shalt thou find in me.

"But at the first thou shalt not attain to them without some sorrow and a laborious conflict.

"Cold inbred habits will resist, but they shall be overcome by better habits.

"The flesh will murmur against thee, but with fervor of spirit it shall be bridled.

"The old Serpent will incite and embitter thee, but will be put to flight by prayer; moreover, by useful employment his entrance will be greatly obstructed."

CHAPTER XII
Of the Obedience of One in Humble Subjection after the Example of Jesus Christ

"My son.

"He who striveth to withdraw himself from obedience withdraweth himself from grace.

"And he who seeketh for himself private gain loseth those which are common to all.

"He who doth not gladly and willingly subject himself to his superior showeth that his flesh doth not yet completely obey him, but often resisteth and murmureth.

"Learn thou therefore quickly to subject thyself

21—Psalms, XXXVII, 4.

to thy superior, if thou desire to keep thine own flesh under the yoke.

"For quickly will the outward enemy overcome, if the inward man hath not been laid low.

"There is no enemy more troublesome and harmful to the soul than thou art to thyself, if thou be not well in harmony with the spirit.

"Thou must wholly adopt a true contempt for thyself, if thou desire to prevail against flesh and blood.

"Because as yet thou lovest thyself too inordinately, therefore thou art afraid to resign thyself wholly to the will of others.

"And yet what great matter is it, if thou, who art dust and nothing, subject thyself to a man for God's sake, when I, the Almighty and the Most High, who created all things of nothing, subjected myself to man for thy sake?

"I became of all men the most humble and the most abject, in order to overcome thy pride with my humility.

"Learn to be obedient, O dust; learn to humble thyself, thou earth and clay, and to bow thyself down under the feet of all men.

"Learn to break thy will, and to yield to every form of subjection.

"Burn with anger against thyself, and let no pride dwell in thee; but show thyself so humble and small that all may be able to walk over thee and tread thee down as the mud of the streets.

"What hast thou to complain of, vain man; what canst thou, vile sinner, answer to them that upbraid thee, thou who hast so often offended God, and so many times deserved hell?

"But my eye spared thee, because thy soul was

precious in my sight, that thou mightst know my love and ever be thankful for my benefits, and that thou give thyself to true subjection and humility, and endure patiently contempt of thyself."

CHAPTER XIII.[22]
How We Must Stand and Speak in Everything That We Desire

"My son.

"Speak thou thus in every matter.

" 'Lord, if it please thee, let this come to pass.

" 'Lord, if this be to thy honor, let it be done in thy name.

" 'Lord, if thou see it is good for me, then grant to me that I may use it to thine honor.

" 'But if thou know it will be harmful to me and of no profit to the salvation of my soul, then take away such a desire from me.'

"For not every desire is of the Holy Spirit, even though it seem unto a man right and good.

"It is difficult to judge truly whether a good spirit or a hostile one impel thee to desire this or that, or whether thou art moved by thine own spirit.

"Many have been deceived in the end, who at the first seemed to be led by a good spirit.

"Therefore whatever occurs to the mind as desirable must always be desired and prayed for in the fear of God and humility of heart, and most of all should one commit the whole matter to me with resignation of self, and say:

" 'O Lord, thou knowest what is best for us; let this or that be done as thou wilt.

" 'Give what thou wilt, and how much thou wilt, and when thou wilt.

22—Thomas a Kempis inserts another chapter.

" 'Deal with me as thou wilt, and as it pleases thee, and is most for thine honor.

" 'Set me where thou wilt, and freely work thy will with me in all things.

" 'I am in thy hand; turn me around: for I long to live not unto myself, but unto thee; and that I might do it worthily and perfectly!' " [23]

CHAPTER XIV
*That True
Solace Is to
Be Sought in
God Alone*

Whatsoever I can desire or imagine for my consolation, I look for it not here but hereafter.

If I alone had all the solaces of the world and could enjoy all pleasures, it is certain that they would not last long.

Wherefore, O my soul, you cannot be fully comforted and wholly refreshed, except in God, the Comforter of the poor and Patron of the humble.

Wait a little while, my soul, wait for the divine promise, and you will have abundance of all good things in heaven.

If you desire inordinately the things present, you will lose those which are heavenly and eternal.

Temporal things are to be in the use, eternal things in the desire.

You cannot be satisfied with any temporal goods, because you are not created to enjoy them.

Although you possessed all created good, you could not be happy and blessed; but in God, who has created all things, consists your whole blessedness and happiness; not such as is seen and commended by the foolish lovers of the world, but such as the good and faithful servants of Christ wait for, and of

23—Thomas a Kempis adds a prayer.

which the spiritual and pure in heart, whose conversation is in heaven, sometimes have a foretaste.

Vain and brief is all human solace.

Blessed and true is the solace that is received inwardly from the Truth.

A devout man carries everywhere about him Jesus, his Comforter, and says to him:

"Be thou present with me, Lord Jesus, in every time and place.

"Let it be my consolation gladly to do without all human comfort." [24]

CHAPTER XV
Of Bearing Injuries and Who Shall be Approved as Truly Patient

"What sayest thou, my son?

"Cease to complain and consider my suffering and that of my saints.

"Thou hast not yet resisted unto blood. [25]

"It is little which thou sufferest, in comparison with those who have suffered so much, have been so strongly tempted, so grievously afflicted, so many ways tried and troubled.

"Thou oughtst therefore to call to mind the more heavy sufferings of others, that thou mayst bear more easily thy lesser ones.

"And if they do not seem very small to thee, then beware lest thy impatience be the cause of this.

"But whether they be small or whether they be great, endeavor patiently to undergo them all.

"The better thou disposest thyself to suffering, the more wisely thou actest, and the greater reward shalt thou receive; thou wilt also more easily endure

24—Thomas a Kempis adds two sentences and two chapters.
25—Hebrews, XII, 4.

it, if thou trainest thy mind and habit not carelessly thereunto.

"And say not, 'I cannot bear these things from such a man, nor are things of this sort to be borne by me, for he hath done me great harm and reproacheth me for things of which I never thought; but from another I would gladly bear them, and in so faɪ as I see that they should be borne.'

"Foolish is such a thought, for it considereth not the power of patience, nor by whom that virtue is to be crowned, but much more it weigheth the persons and the injuries inflicted on him.

"He is not truly patient who is willing to suffer only as much as he thinketh good, and from whom he pleaseth.

"But the truly patient man considereth not by what man he is tried, whether by his superior, or by one of his equals, or by an inferior; whether by a good and holy man, or by one who is perverse and unworthy; but indifferently from every creature, whatsoever or how often soever adversity befall him, he taketh it all thankfully as from the hands of God, and counteth it great gain; for with God nothing which is borne for his sake, however small, shall pass without its reward.

"Be therefore prepared for the fight, if thou wilt have the victory.

"Without a combat thou canst not attain to the crown of patience.

"If thou wilt not suffer, thou refusest to be crowned." [26]

26—Thomas a Kempis adds six sentences and two chapters.

CHAPTER XVI
Of the Remembrance of God's Manifold Benefits

Open, O Lord, my heart in thy law, and teach me to walk in the way of thy commandments.

Grant me to understand thy will, and with great reverence and diligent meditation to remember thy benefits, both general and special, that henceforth I may be able worthily to give thee thanks.

Yet I know and confess that I am not able, even in the least point, to render thee due thanks for the favors which thou bestowest upon me.

I am less than the least of all the good things which thou gavest me, and when I consider thy majesty, my spirit fainteth because of the greatness thereof.

All that we have in soul and in body, and whatever we possess outwardly or inwardly, naturally or supernaturally, are thy good gifts.[27]

Although one have received more, another less, yet all are thine, and without thee one cannot have even the least blessing.

He who hath received the greatest cannot glory of his own merit, nor extol himself above others, nor despise those beneath him; because he is the greater and the better who ascribeth least to himself, and in thanksgiving is more humble and devout.

And he who considereth himself more lowly than all others, and despiseth himself as more unworthy, is more apt to receive the greater blessings.

But he who hath received less should not be sad and not bear it unwillingly, and not envy those who are richer.[28]

27—Thomas a Kempis has a longer sentence.
28—Thomas a Kempis has a longer sentence.

All things proceed from thee; therefore in all thou art to be praised.

Thou knowest what is fit to be given to every one; and why this man should have less and that one more, is not for us but for thee to judge.

Therefore, O Lord and God, I esteem it a great benefit that I do not have much of that which outwardly and in the opinion of men seemeth worthy of praise and honor; for so it is that he who considereth his own poverty and vileness should not only draw therefrom no grief or sorrow, or sadness of spirit, but rather comfort and great joy; because thou, O God, hast chosen the poor and humble, and those despised by the world, to be thy friends and companions.

Witnesses are thy apostles, whom thou hast made princes over all the earth.

And yet they lived in the world without complaint, so humble and simple, without all malice and deceit, that they even rejoiced to suffer reproach for thy name; and what the world abhorreth, they embraced with great affection.

Therefore nothing ought so much to make him rejoice, who loveth thee, and knoweth thy benefits, as thy will in him, and the good pleasure of thy eternal appointment; and with this he ought to be so contented and comforted that he would be as willingly the least as another would wish to be the greatest, and just as satisfied and content in the last place as in the first; as willing to be despised and abased, of no name and character, as to be more honorable and great in the world than others.

For thy will and the love of thy glory ought to be preferred before all things, and to comfort and please one more than all the benefits that have been given or can be given to him.

CHAPTER XVII
*Of Four Things
That Bring
Great Peace*

"My son, now I will teach thee the way of peace and true liberty.[29]

"Be desirous, my son, to do the will of another rather than thine own.

"Choose always to have less rather than more.

"Seek always the lowest place, and to be inferior to every one.

"Wish always that the will of God be wholly fulfilled in thee.

"Behold, such a man entereth within the borders of peace and rest."

O Lord, this short discourse of thine containeth within itself much perfection.

It is short in words but full of meaning and abundant in fruit.

For if it could be faithfully kept by me, I ought not so easily to be disturbed.

For as often as I feel myself discontented and weighed down, I find that I have deviated from this doctrine. [30]

CHAPTER XVIII
*Of Avoiding
Curious Inquiry
into the Life
of Another*

"My son, be not curious, nor trouble thyself with idle anxieties.

"What is this or that to thee? Follow thou me.[31]

"For what is it to thee, whether that man be this or that, or whether this man speak this or that?

29—Thomas a Kempis inserts an awkward interruption.
30—Thomas a Kempis adds one sentence and two prayers.
31—John, XXI, 22.

"Thou shalt not need to answer for others, but shalt give account for thyself.

"Why therefore dost thou entangle thyself?

"Behold, I know every one, and do see all things that are done under the sun; also I know how it is with every one, what he thinketh, what he wisheth, and at what his intentions aim.

"Unto me therefore are all things to be committed, but do thou keep thyself gently at peace, and let each one do as he pleaseth.

"Whatsoever he shall do or say shall come unto him, for he cannot deceive me.

"Do not trouble thyself about the shadow of a great name, or about the friendship of many, nor about the private affection of men.

"For these things bring distraction, and great darkness in the heart.

"I would gladly speak my word and reveal to thee my secrets, if thou wouldst diligently observe my coming, and open unto me the door of thine heart.

"Be thou circumspect and watch in prayer, and humble thyself in all things."

CHAPTER XIX
*Wherein Firm
Peace of Heart
and True
Progress
Consist*

"My son.

"I have said, 'Peace I leave with you, my peace I give unto you; not as the world giveth, give I unto you.' [32]

"Peace is what all desire, but all do not care for the things that pertain to true peace.

"My peace is with the humble and gentle of heart.

32—John. XIV. 27.

"Thy peace shall be in great patience.

"If thou wilt hear me and follow my voice, thou shalt enjoy great peace."

What then shall I do, Lord?

"In every matter look to thyself, what thou doest and what thou sayest; and direct thy whole attention unto this that thou mayst please me alone, and neither desire nor seek anything besides me; but of the words and deeds of others judge nothing rashly; neither do thou entangle thyself with things not committed to thee, and doing thus thou mayst be little or seldom disturbed.

"But never to feel any disturbance at all, nor to suffer any trouble of mind or body, belongs not to this life, but to the state of eternal rest.

"Think not that thou hast found true peace, if thou feel no burden; nor that then all is well, if thou art vexed with no adversary, nor that 'to be perfect' is to have all things done according to desire; and do thou then not think thyself something great, nor reckon thyself specially beloved, if thou art filled with devotion and sweetness; for it is not by these things that a true lover of virtue is known, nor do progress and perfection of a man consist in these things."

Wherein then, O Lord?

"In giving thyself over with all thy heart to the Divine Will, not seeking things that are thine own, whether great or small, whether temporal or eternal; so that thou shalt keep the same countenance in giving of thanks, both in prosperity and adversity, weighing all things in an equal balance.

"If thou be so brave and persevering in hope, that thou after the withdrawal of inner comfort prepare thy heart to suffer even greater things; and if thou do not justify thyself, as if thou oughtst not to suffer such grievous things, but justify me in whatsoever I appoint, and praise my holy name, then thou walkest in the true and right way of peace, and shalt have a sure hope that thou shalt again behold my face with great delight.

"For if thou attain to the full contempt of thyself, know that thou shalt then enjoy abundance of peace, as much as is possible to thy state of pilgrimage."

CHAPTER XX [33]
*That Personal
Love Hinders
Most from the
Highest Good*

"My son.

"Thou must give all for all, and be nothing of thine own.

"Know that the love of thyself doth thee more hurt than anything in the world.

"According to the love and the inclination which thou hast, so doth everything more or less cleave to thee.

"If thy love be pure, simple, and well ordered, thou shalt be free from the bondage of things.

"Do not covet that which thou mayst not have.

"Do not have that which may hinder thee and rob thee of inward freedom.

"It is strange that thou committest not thyself wholly unto me, from the bottom of thy heart, with all things that thou canst have or desire.

"Why dost thou consume thyself with vain grief? Why weary thyself with superfluous cares?

"Stand by my good pleasure, and thou shalt suffer no loss.

"If thou seek this or that, and wouldst be in such

33—Thomas a Kempis adds one chapter.

and such a place, the better to enjoy thine own profit and pleasure, thou shalt never be at rest and free from care; for in everything there will be some flaw, and in every place something unpleasant.

"Therefore it is of no benefit if one obtain and multiply external things, but rather if one despise them and root them out from the heart.

"This thou must not understand of money and riches only, but also of striving after honor and of seeking vain praise, all of which passeth away with the world." [34]

CHAPTER XXI
Against Slander

"My son.

"Take it not grievously if some think ill of thee, and speak that which thou wouldst not gladly hear.

"Thou oughtst to think worse of thyself, and to believe no one weaker than thyself.

"If thou walkest inwardly, thou wilt not weigh much the fleeting words.

"It is no small prudence to keep silence in an evil time, and inwardly to turn thyself to me, and not to be troubled by human judgment.

"Let not thy peace depend upon the tongues of men.

"For whether they interpret well or ill of thee, thou art not therefore another man.

"Where is true peace and true honor?

"Is it not in me?

"And he who desiretn not to please men, nor feareth to displease, shall enjoy abundant peace.

"From inordinate love and vain fear arise all disquietness of heart and distraction of the senses."

34—Thomas a Kempis adds two sentences and a prayer.

CHAPTER XXII [35]
*Of Asking for
Divine Aid,
and the
Confidence of
Recovering
Grace*

"My son.

"I am the Lord, who giveth strength in the day of need.

"Come unto me when it is not well with thee.

"This it is which most of all hindereth heavenly consolation, that thou art too slow in turning thyself unto prayer.

"For before thou dost earnestly pray to me, thou seekest in the meantime many means of comfort, and refreshest thyself in outward things.

"And so it cometh to pass that all things profit thee little, until thou note that it is I who deliver those that trust in me, and that outside me there is neither powerful help nor profitable counsel nor lasting remedy; but do thou now recover courage after the tempest, grow strong again in the light of mercy, for I am nigh, saith the Lord, to repair all, not only with no decrease, but abundantly and in a plentiful measure.

"Is there anything hard for me, or shall I be like one who saith and doeth not?

"Where is thy faith?

"Stand firmly and with perseverance.

"Be long-suffering and brave; comfort will come to thee in due time.

"Wait for me, wait; I will come and take care of thee.

"It is a temptation that vexeth thee, and a vain fear that frighteneth thee.

"What bringeth anxiety about future events, but that thou hast sorrow upon sorrow?

35—Thomas a Kempis adds one chapter.

"Sufficient for the day is the evil thereof.[36]

"It is a vain thing and unprofitable to be either disturbed or pleased about future events which perhaps will never come to pass.

"But it is the nature of man to be deceived by fancies of this sort, and a sign of a soul as yet small, to be so easily led astray by the suggestions of the enemy.

"For it is immaterial to him whether he deceive or delude by real or imaginary means; whether he cause one to fall with a love of present, or a fear of future things.

"Let not therefore thy heart be troubled, neither let it fear.

"Trust in me, and put thy confidence in my mercy.

"When thou thinkest thyself farthest away from me, I am often nearest unto thee.

"When thou reckonest that almost all is lost, then the gain of great reward is often close at hand.

"Not all is lost, when something falleth out contrary to thy wishes.

"Thou oughtst not to judge according to present feeling, nor so to take or give way to any grief which befalleth thee, as if all hope of escape were taken away.

"Do not consider thyself wholly forsaken, when I for a time send thee some tribulation, or even withdraw the desired comforts.

"For in this way one entereth the kingdom of heaven.

"And this is undoubtedly more profitable for thee and my other servants, that ye be tried with adversi-

36—Matthew, VI, 34.

ties, than that ye had everything according to your desires.

"I know the hidden thoughts; for it is very expedient for thy welfare that occasionally thou art left without relish, lest perchance thou shouldst be puffed up with thy prosperity, and pleased with thyself for that which thou art not.

"That which I have given I can take away, and restore when I please.

"When I give it, it is mine; when I withdraw it, I do not take what is thine; for mine is every good gift and every perfect gift.

"When I send upon thee any affliction or any cross, do not be angry, and let not thy courage fail; I can quickly raise up, and change heaviness into joy.

"But I am always just, and greatly to be praised, when I deal thus with thee.

"If thou hast the right insight, and considerest what the truth is, thou wilt never mourn dejectedly for any adversity which befalleth thee; but rather rejoice and give thanks therefor; yet thou wilt account this thy special joy, that I afflict thee with sorrows, and do not spare thee.

"As my father hath loved me, I also love you, [37] said I to my disciples, whom I certainly sent not out to temporal joys, but to great conflicts; not to honors, but to shame; not to leisure, but to labor; not to rest, but to bring forth much fruit with patience." [38]

37—John, XV, 9.
38—Thomas a Kempis adds five words.

CHAPTER XXIII
*Of the
Neglect of All
Creatures that
the Creator
May Be Found*

O Lord, I still need more grace, if I would arrive where neither man nor any creature may hinder me.

For as long as anything holdeth me back, I cannot freely fly to thee.

To fly freely desired he who said, "Oh, that I had wings like a dove, for then would I flee away and be at rest." [39]

What is more at rest than a single eye?

And what is more free than he who desireth nothing on earth?

Therefore must one mount over all creatures, and perfectly forsake himself, and stand firmly with abstracted mind, and see that thou the Creator of all hast nothing among creatures like unto thyself.

And unless one be disengaged from creatures, he cannot freely attend to divine things.

Therefore few are found who contemplate God, because few know how to withdraw themselves wholly from perishing and created things.

For this much grace is necessary, which may lift up the soul, and carry it away above itself.

And unless a person is elevated in spirit, and freed from all creatures, and wholly united unto God, whatsoever he knoweth, whatsoever also he hath, it is of no great weight.

For a long time shall he be small and lie low, who esteemeth anything great save the One, Infinite, Eternal Good.

And whatsoever is not God is nothing, and ought to be accounted as nothing. [40]

39—Psalms, LV, 6.
40—Thomas a Kempis adds two sentences.

Many are found who long for the contemplation of God, but do not take pains to practise those things which are required thereunto.

It is a great hindrance that one rest in signs and sensible things, and applies himself too little to complete mortification.

I know not what it is, or by what spirit we are led, or what aim we have, that we who would be deemed spiritual devote so much pains and even more anxiety to perishable and mean things, while we very seldom think of our inward selves, with full recollection of mind.

Alas, we forthwith, after a little recollection, drift to outward things again, and do not weigh our deeds with strict examination.

We mind not where our affections lie, and do not complain because everything is so unclean in our actions.

For all flesh had corrupted itself upon the earth,[41] and therefore the great deluge followed.

Since, then, our inward affections are very corrupt, our actions thence proceeding must needs be corrupted also.[42]

From a pure heart proceedeth the fruit of a good life.

We ask how much a man hath accomplished, but from what degree of virtuous principle he acteth is not so carefully weighed.

We inquire whether he hath been brave, rich, handsome, skilful, a good writer, a good singer, or a good laborer; but how poor he is in spirit, how

41—Genesis, VI, 12.
42—Thomas a Kempis adds, "being the index of a deficient inward strength."

patient and meek, how devout and spiritual, on these things many are silent.

Nature respecteth the outward appearance of man; grace turneth itself to the inward man.

The former is frequently deceived; the latter trusteth in God so that it may not be deluded.

CHAPTER XXIV
Of Self-Denial and the Renunciation of Every Evil Appetite

"My son, thou canst not possess perfect liberty unless thou wholly renounce thyself.

"They are all in fetters who seek their own interests and are lovers of themselves, covetous, inquisitive, gossiping, always seeking what is pleasant, not the things of Jesus Christ, but often devising and framing that which will not last.

"For everything will perish that is not of God.

"Keep this short and complete saying.

" 'Forsake all and thou shalt find all. Renounce thy lust and thou shalt attain rest.'

"Weigh this, and when thou hast fulfilled it, thou shalt understand all things."

O Lord, this is not the work of a single day, and no child's play; yea, rather in this short word is included all the perfection of devout persons.

"My son, thou oughtst not to turn away and not at once be cast down when thou hearest of the way of the perfect; but shouldst rather be stirred up to higher things; and at least in deep longing sigh after them.

"Oh, that it were so with thee, and that thou hadst arrived at this, that thou wert not a lover of thyself, but wert always ready at the call of my word and that of my Father; [43] then shouldst thou please me greatly, and thy whole life would pass in joy and peace.

"Thou hast yet many things to renounce, and unless thou wholly resign them to me, thou shalt not attain to that which thou desirest.

"I counsel thee to buy of me gold tried in the fire; that thou mayst be rich,[44] that is heavenly wisdom, which treadeth underfoot all that is here below.

"Leave behind thee all earthly wisdom, all that is pleasant to human beings and to thee.

"I said that thou must buy vile things with those which are costly and great in the minds of men, for very mean, of small account, and almost forgotten among men doth true heavenly wisdom appear, which thinketh not highly of itself, nor seeketh to be praised on earth, which many only praise with their lips, while in their lives they are far from it; nevertheless it is the precious pearl which is hidden from many."

CHAPTER XXV
Of the Instability of the Heart and of Directing the Final Aim toward God

"My son, trust not thy feeling as it is at present; it will quickly be changed into something else.

"As long as thou livest, thou art subject to change, even against thy will; so that thou wilt be found now joyful, now sad; now at peace, now disquieted; now

43—Thomas a Kempis has, "and of him whom I have placed over thee as a father," which is probably an error.

44—Revelation, III, 18.

devout, now indevout; now diligent, now listless; now grave, now flippant.

"But above these changeable moods standeth he who is wise and well instructed in spirit; who is not attentive to what he feeleth in himself, or which way the wind of instability bloweth; but to this, that the whole intention of his mind is turned to the right and desired aim.

"For thus will he be able to remain one and the same and unshaken, if in the midst of so many various events he keepeth the single eye fixed unceasingly upon me.

"The purer the eye of the intention is, the more securely doth one pass through the different storms.

"But in many the eye of pure intention is dim, for it quickly is turned away to something pleasant which it seeketh; and rarely findeth one somebody who is quite free from the fetters of self-seeking.

"So of old the Jews came to Bethany to Martha and Mary, not for Jesus' sake only, but that they might see Lazarus also.

"One ought to purge the eye of the intention, that it may be single and right, and to direct it toward me, beyond all the various objects that may come between."

CHAPTER XXVI
That God Is Sweet above All Things and in All Things to Him Who Loves Him

Behold, my God and my all!

What more will I, and what more blessed thing can I desire?

O lovely and sweet word! but only to him who loveth the word, not the world nor the things that are in the world.

My God and my all!

To him who understandeth, enough is said.[45]

When thou art present, all things are delightful; but when thou art absent, everything is disagreeable.

Thou makest a quiet heart and great peace and festive joy.

Thou causest us to think well of everything and to praise thee in everything, neither can anything please long without thee, but if it is to be agreeable and satisfy, thy grace must be present, and it must be seasoned with the seasoning of thy wisdom.

What will not be tasteful to him who hath a relish for thee?

And he who hath no relish for thee, what shall be able to give him joy?

But the wise men of the world, and those who are carnally minded, fail in thy wisdom; for among the worldly-wise is found very great vanity, and among the carnally minded, death.

But they who follow thee by the contempt of worldly things, and the mortification of the flesh, are known to be truly wise, because they turn themselves from vanity to truth, from flesh to spirit.

Those relish God; and all the good that is found in creatures, they refer wholly unto the praise of their Maker.

Unlike, yea, very unlike, are the enjoyment of the Creator and of the creation, of eternity and of time, of the uncreated light and the reflected light.[46]

45—Thomas a Kempis has a longer sentence.
46—Thomas a Kempis adds a long passage.

CHAPTER XXVII
*That There Is
No Security
from Temp-
tation in
This Life*
"My son.

"Never art thou secure in this life, but as long as thou livest thou shalt need spiritual armor.

"Thou dwellest among enemies, and on the right and on the left thou art attacked.

"If therefore thou defend not thyself on all sides with the shield of patience, thou wilt not be long without a wound.

"Moreover, if thou keep not thy heart fixed upon me with sincere desire to suffer all things for me, thou wilt not be able to bear the heat of this combat, nor to attain the victor's palm of the blessed.

"Thou must also manfully pass through all, and bare a strong hand against opposition.

"For to him that overcometh is the hidden manna given, but for the indolent remaineth much misery.

"If thou seek rest in this life, how wilt thou then attain the everlasting Rest?

"Dispose not thy mind for much rest, but for great patience.

"Do not seek the true peace on earth, but in heaven; not in men, nor in any other creatures, but in God alone.

"For the love of God thou oughtst cheerfully to undergo all things; that is to say, labors and sorrows, temptations, vexations, anxiety, necessity, illness, injustice, contradiction, rebuke, humiliation, shame, correction, and scorn.

"These help in virtue, these protect the novice in Christ, these prepare the heavenly crown.

"I will give eternal reward for brief labor, and infinite glory for transitory shame.

"Thinkest thou that thou shalt always have spiritual consolations at thine own will?

"My saints did not always have such, but many afflictions and manifold temptations and heavy desolations.

"But patiently they bore themselves in all, and trusted God more than themselves, knowing that the sufferings of this present time are not worthy to merit the future glory.

"Wilt thou have that at once, which many after many tears and heavy labors have hardly obtained?

"Wait for the Lord, act as a man, and be strong; be not faint-hearted, nor give way, but steadfastly devote body and soul to the glory of God.

"I will reward it in fullest measure; I will be with thee in trouble." [47]

CHAPTER XXVIII   "My son.
*Against
the Vain*   "Cast thy heart firmly on the
Judgments   Lord, and fear not human judgment,
of Men   when conscience pronounceth thee upright and innocent.

"It is good and blessed thus to suffer, and that will not be grievous to the humble heart, which trusteth God more than itself.

"Many people say different things, and therefore little trust is to be placed in them.

"Moreover to satisfy all is not possible.

"Although Paul took pains to please all in the Lord, and became all things to all men,[48] yet with

47—Psalms, XCI, 15.
48—I Corinthians, IX, 22.

him it was a small thing that he should be judged
by man's judgment.[49]

"He did enough for the edification and salvation
of others, as much as lay in his power; but he could
not avoid being sometimes judged and often despised
by others.

"Therefore he committed all to God, who knew
all; and by patience and humility defended himself
against men who spoke unjust things or thought
vanities and lies, and brought accusations as they
pleased.

"Sometimes, however, he made answer, lest the
weak were offended by his silence.

"Who art thou, that thou shouldst fear a mortal
man? [50]

"To-day he is here, and to-morrow he is not seen.

"Fear God, and thou shalt not quail before the
terrors of men.

"What can one man do against thee with words
or injuries?

"He hurteth himself more than thee, and he shall
not be able to escape the judgment of God, whoever
he may be.

"Have thou God before thine eyes, and do not
contend with fretful words.

"And if for the present thou seem to be worsted,
and to suffer shame undeservedly, do not therefore
grow angry, and do not lessen thy crown by impatience; but rather lift up thine eyes unto me in
heaven, who am able to deliver thee from all shame
and injury, and to reward every man according to
his works."

49—I Corinthians, IV, 3.
50—Isaiah, LI, 12.

CHAPTER XXIX
*Of Pure
and Entire
Resignation of
Self, for
Obtaining
Liberty
of Heart*

"My son.

"Forsake thyself, and thou shalt find me.

"Stand still, without choice of thine own and all thoughts of self, and thou shalt ever gain.

"For richer grace shall be added unto thee, as soon as thou resignest thyself, and dost not turn back to thyself again."

O Lord, how often shall I resign myself, and in what things shall I lose myself?

"Always; every hour; in small matters as in great.

"I except nothing, but desire that I shall find thee naked in all things.

"Otherwise how canst thou be mine and I thine, if thou be not stripped inwardly and outwardly of all self-will?

"The sooner thou dost this, the better it will be with thee; and the more fully and sincerely, the more thou shalt please me, and the richer reward shalt thou have.

"Some resign themselves, but with certain exceptions, for they do not fully trust in God; hence they endeavor to provide for themselves.

"Some also at first offer all, but afterward, being pressed by temptation, they return to their own devices, wherefore they make little progress in virtue.

"These shall not attain to the true liberty of the pure heart, and to the grace of my sweet friendship; unless they first make an entire resignation and daily offer themselves as a sacrifice, without which there neither is nor can be any blissful union.

"I have often said to thee, and now I say it again.

"Forsake thyself, resign thyself, and thou shalt enjoy great inward peace.

"Give all for all, except nothing, require back nothing, attach thyself wholly and unswervingly to me, and thou shalt have me.

"Thou shalt be free in heart, and darkness shall not oppress thee.

"Strive for this, pray for this, long for this, that thou mayst be stripped of all self-seeking, and nakedly follow Jesus; mayst die to thyself, and live eternally to me.

"Then shall all vain fancies vanish, all groundless disturbances, all superfluous cares.

"Then also immoderate fear shall depart, and inordinate love shall die."

CHAPTER XXX
Of Proper Control in External Things and Recourse to God in Dangers

"My son.

"Thou must conscientiously endeavor that thou in every place and in every action or external employment mayst be inwardly free and thoroughly master of thyself; and that all things be under thee, and thou not under them; that thou be lord and ruler of thine actions, not a slave and hireling, but rather a freed man and a true Hebrew passing over into the lot and freedom of the sons of God, who stand above the present and look upon the eternal, who with the left eye behold things transitory, and with the right eye, heavenly; whom temporal things draw not nor cleave unto, but they rather draw temporal things to themselves to make them serve properly as ordained and approved by God, who hath left nothing without order in his creation.

"If thou also dost not in every circumstance turn thyself to outward appearances, and dost not judge with a carnal eye what thou seest or hearest, but straitway in every cause enterest with Moses the tabernacle to ask counsel of the Lord, thou shalt sometimes hear the divine answer and return instructed in things that are and shall be.

"For Moses always had recourse to the tabernacle for the solving of all doubts and questions, and fled to the help of prayer in order to bear more easily the dangers and the iniquity of men.

"Thus oughtst thou also to flee into the secret chamber of thy heart, to implore more earnestly the divine succor.

"For this cause, as we read,[51] were Joshua and the children of Israel deceived by the Gibeonites, because they asked not beforehand counsel of the Lord."

CHAPTER XXXI
That Man Must Not Be Impatient in His Occupation

"My son.

"Always commit thy cause to me; I will dispose it well in due time.

"Wait for my ordering of it, and thou shalt find it for thy profit.[52]

"My son.

"A man often striveth vehemently after something he desireth, but when he hath obtained it he beginneth to think differently of it; for the desires are not permanently intent on the same thing, but rush from one thing to another.

"It is therefore no small matter to forsake self even in the smallest things.

51—Joshua, IX, 14.
52—Thomas a Kempis adds two sentences.

"The true progress of man consisteth in the denial of himself.

"And a man who denieth himself is quite free and secure.

"But the old enemy, who opposeth all good things, ceaseth not from tempting, but day and night lieth grievously in wait, to cast the unwary into the snare of deceit.

" 'Watch and pray,' saith the Lord, 'lest ye enter into temptation.' " [53]

CHAPTER XXXII
*That Man Has
No Good in
Himself, and
Nothing
Whereof
He Can Glory*

Lord, what is man, that thou art mindful of him? [54]

What hath man deserved, that thou shouldst grant him grace?

Lord, what cause can I have to complain if thou forsake me? [55]

I have no good in myself, but in all things I am defective, and ever tend to nothing.

And if I am not helped by thee, and inwardly strengthened, I become altogether lukewarm and reckless.

But thou, Lord, art always the same and endurest forever; always good, just, and holy; doing all things well, justly, and holily, and ordering them in wisdom; but I, who am more ready to go backward than forward, do not always continue in one estate, for seven times are passed over me.

Nevertheless it quickly becometh better when it so pleaseth thee and thou stretchest forth thy helping hand; for thou alone canst help me without human

53—Matthew, XXVI, 41.
54—Psalms, VIII, 4; Thomas a Kempis has a longer quotation.
55—Thomas a Kempis adds one sentence.

aid, and so strengthen me that my countenance shall change no more, but that my heart shall turn itself to thee, and be at rest in thee alone.

Wherefore if I but knew well how to reject all human consolation, either for the attaining of devotion, or because of the necessity by which I am forced to seek thee, because there is no man who can comfort me, then could I properly and justly trust in thy grace, and rejoice in the gift of new consolation.

Thanks be unto thee, from whom all proceedeth, whenever it goeth well with me.

But I am in thy sight mere vanity and nothing, a vacillating and weak man.

Of what then can I glory, or for what do I desire to be respected?

Is it for naught?

This also is utterly vain.

Verily, empty glory is an evil pest, and a very great vanity, because it draweth a man from true glory, and robbeth him of heavenly grace.

For while man pleaseth himself, he displeaseth thee; while he craveth human praise, he is deprived of true virtues.

But true glory and holy rejoicing is for a man to glory in thee, and not in himself; to take no delight in any creature, except for thy sake.

Praised be thy name, not mine; magnified be thy work, not mine; let thy holy name be blessed, but to me let nothing be given of the praises of men.

Thou art my glory; thou art the joy of my heart; in thee will I glory and rejoice all the day, but as for myself, I will not glory save only in mine infirmities.

Let the Jews seek the honor which cometh from one another; I will seek that which cometh from God only.[56]

All human glory, all temporal honor, all worldly eminence, compared with thy eternal glory, is vanity and folly.

O my Truth and my Mercy, my God, blessed Trinity; unto thee alone be praise, honor, strength, and glory for ever and ever.

CHAPTER XXXIII
Of the
Contempt of
All Temporal
Honor

"My son, make it no matter of thine, if thou see others honored and exalted, but thyself despised and humbled.

"Lift up thy heart to me in heaven, and the contempt of men on earth will not grieve thee."

O Lord, we are in blindness, and are quickly misled by vanity.

If I look rightly into myself, never was injustice done to me by any creature; wherefore I am not justified in complaining before thee.

But because I have often and grievously sinned against thee, all creatures do justly arm themselves against me.

To me, therefore, shame and contempt are justly due; but unto thee, praise, honor, and glory.

And if I do not prepare myself gladly to be despised and forsaken of all creatures, and to be esteemed altogether as nothing, I cannot be inwardly filled with peace and strength, nor spiritually enlightened, nor fully united with thee.

56—John, V, 44.

CHAPTER XXXIV
That Peace Is Not to Be Placed in Men

"My son.

"If thou place thy peace on the relation with any person because thou agreest and livest with him, thou shalt be unstable and disquiet.

"But if thou have recourse to the ever living and abiding Truth, the desertion or death of a friend shall not grieve thee.

"In me ought the love of thy friend be grounded, and for my sake oughtst thou to love him who appeareth to thee good, and very dear in this life.

"Without me friendship hath no strength, no endurance; neither is that love true and pure which I unite not.

"Thou oughtst to be so dead to such affections of beloved humans that, as far as in thee lieth, thou wouldst choose to be without all human companionship.

"So much the nearer doth man approach God, the farther he retireth from earthly comfort.

"So much the higher he ascendeth toward God, the deeper he descendeth into himself, and the meaner he is in his own sight.

"But he who attributeth any good to himself hindereth the grace of God from coming to him, because the grace of the Holy Spirit ever seeketh a humble heart.

"If thou couldst but perfectly esteem thyself as naught, and but free thyself from all inordinate love, then would I overflow into thee with great grace.

"When thou lookest to creatures, the countenance of the Creator is withdrawn from thee.

"Learn in all things to overcome thyself for the

sake of the Creator; then shalt thou be able to attain to divine knowledge.

"How small soever anything be, if it be loved and regarded inordinately, it holdeth thee back from the highest good, and corrupteth."

CHAPTER XXXV
*Against Vain
and Worldly
Knowledge*

"My son.

"Let not the fair and subtle sayings of men move thee.

"For the Kingdom of God consisteth not in word, but in power.[57]

"Give attention to my words, which inflame the heart and enlighten the mind; they bring contrition and supply manifold consolations.

"Never read thou a word in order to appear more learned and more wise.

"Strive for the mortification of thy sins, for this will profit thee more than the knowledge of many difficult questions.

"When thou hast read and learned many things, thou must always return to the one first principle.

"I am he who teacheth men knowledge, and I bestow on little children a clearer understanding than can be taught by man.

"He to whom I speak shall quickly be wise, and shall grow much in the spirit.

"Woe be to them who inquire many curious things of men, and take little care about the way of serving me.

"The time shall come when the Teacher of Teachers, Christ, the Lord of angels, shall appear to hear the lessons of all, that is, to examine the consciences of each one; and then he shall search Jerusalem with

57—I Corinthians, IV, 20.

candles,[58] and the hidden things of darkness shall be made manifest, and the arguings of men's tongues shall be silent.

"I am he who exalteth in a moment the humble mind, to comprehend more reasonings of the Eternal Truth than if one had studied ten years in the schools.

"I teach without the noise of words, without the confusion of opinions, without the darkness of ambition, without the clash of arguments.

"I am he who teacheth men to despise worldly things, to scorn things present, to seek things heavenly, to relish things eternal, to flee honors, to endure offenses, to place all hope in me, to desire nothing apart from me, and above all things to love me ardently.

"For a certain person, by loving me from the bottom of his heart, learned divine things, and was able to speak wonderful truths.

"He achieved more by relinquishing all things than by studying subtleties.

"But to some I speak common things, to others special; to some I gently appear in signs and figures, but to others I reveal mysteries in much light.

"The voice of books is one and the same, but it doth not inform all alike, for I am a teacher of truth within man, a searcher of the heart, a discerner of thoughts, a mover of actions, distributing to each one as I deem him worthy."

58—Zephaniah, I, 12.

CHAPTER XXXVI
*Of Not
Troubling
Ourselves
about Out-
ward Things*

"My Son.

"In many things thou oughtst to be ignorant, and to esteem thyself as one dead on earth, and as one to whom the whole world is crucified.

"Many things also thou must pass by with a deaf ear, and must rather think upon those which belong to thy peace.

"It is more profitable to turn away one's eyes from unpleasing subjects, and to leave each person to his own opinions, than to trouble one's self about contentious discourses.

"If thou stand well with God, thou shalt more easily endure a state of subjection."

O Lord, to what have we come?

A temporal loss is bewailed; for a small gain we labor and hurry; and spiritual loss is forgotten, and scarcely do we later recover it.

That which profiteth little or nothing is looked after, and that which is altogether necessary is negligently passed over; because man loseth himself wholly in earthly things.

And if he doth not quickly recover himself, he gladly lieth down in outward things.

CHAPTER XXXVII
*That We Must
Not Believe
Every One and
That We Are
Prone to Go
Wrong in Words*

Lord, be thou my help in need, for vain is the help of man.[59]

How often have I found no faithfulness where I thought I possessed it!

How often, too, have I found it where I had expected it less!

Vain therefore is hope in men.

59—Psalms, LX, 11.

Weak are we and unstable; quickly are we deceived and changed.

Where is the man who is able to keep himself in all things so warily and circumspectly, as not sometimes to come into some deception or perplexity?

But he who trusteth in thee, Lord, and seeketh thee with a single heart, doth not so easily slip.

And if he fall into any tribulation, howsoever he may be entangled, yet very quickly shall he be delivered through thee, or comforted by thee, because thou wilt not forsake him to the end who trusteth in thee.[60]

Why have I so easily trusted in others?

But we are men, and nothing but frail men, even though by many we are reckoned and called angels.

Whom shall I trust, O Lord?

Whom but thee?

Thou art the Truth which deceiveth not and cannot be deceived.

And on the other hand, every man is a liar, weak, unstable, and frail, especially in words; so that one ought scarcely ever to believe that which seemeth to sound rightly.

With what wisdom hast thou warned us beforehand that "the enemies of a man are they of his own household." [61]

"Be cautious," saith some one, "be careful, keep unto thyself what I tell thee."

But he also who hath asked for silence cannot keep silence, but forthwith betrayeth me and himself, while he goeth away.

60—Thomas a Kempis adds seven sentences.
61—Matthew, X, 36.

From such talk and such heedless persons protect me, O Lord, that I fall not into their hands.

Put a true and unchangeable word into my mouth, and remove a deceitful tongue far from me.[62]

Oh, how good it is, and tending to peace, to be silent about other men, and not to believe everything without discrimination, nor too easily to hand on reports, to lay one's self open to few, ever to seek thee as the discerner of the heart, and not to be moved to and fro by the wind of words, but to desire that everything be accomplished according to the good pleasure of thy will!

How safe it is for the keeping of heavenly grace to fly from human approval, and not to long after those things which seem to cause admiration, but to pursue with all diligence the things which bring amendment of life and godly zeal!

How many have been injured for having their virtue known and too hastily commended; how truly profitable hath been grace when preserved in silence in this frail life, which, as we are told, is all temptation and warfare!

CHAPTER XXXVIII
Of Having Confidence in God When Evil Words Are Cast at Us

"My son.

"Stand fast and believe in me.

"For what are words but words?

"They fly through the air but bruise not a stone.

"If thou art guilty, think how thou wouldst gladly amend thyself.

"If thou art conscious of nothing wrong on thy part, consider that thou wouldst gladly suffer this for God's sake.

62—Thomas a Kempis adds one sentence.

"Little enough it is to suffer sometimes from words, since thou art not yet able to endure hard blows.

"And why do such trivial matters go to thy heart, except that thou art still carnal, and regardest men more than thou oughtst?

"For it is because thou fearest to be despised that thou art unwilling to be reproved for thy faults, and seekest the shelter of excuses.

"But look better into thyself, and thou shalt acknowledge that the world is yet alive in thee, and a vain desire to please men.

"For when thou shrinkest from being abased and disgraced for thy faults, it is evident that thou art not yet truly humble, nor truly dead to the world, and that the world is not crucified to thee.

"But harken to my word, and thou shalt not care for ten thousand words spoken by men.

"Behold, if all should be spoken against thee that could be maliciously invented, what would it hurt thee, if thou wouldst suffer it to pass entirely away, and make no more account of it than of a blade of grass?

"Could it pluck out a single hair of thy head?

"But he who hath not turned his heart within, nor hath God before his eyes, is easily moved by a word of reproach.

"Whereas he who trusteth in me, and doth not desire to confide in his own judgment, shall be free from the fear of men.

"For I am the Judge and Discerner of all secrets; I know how the matter passed; I know him who doeth the injury, and him who suffereth it.

"From me went forth that word, by my permission this hath happened, that the thoughts of many hearts may be revealed.[63]

"I shall judge the guilty and the innocent, but by a secret judgment I have willed beforehand to try them both.

"The testimony of men often deceiveth; my judgment is true; it shall stand, and shall not be overthrown.

"It commonly lieth hid, and is manifest in special cases to but few; yet it never erreth, nor can err, although to the eyes of the foolish it may not seem right.

"To me therefore one ought to hasten in every judgment, and not to lean on his own opinion.

"For to the just no evil shall happen, whatever may befall him from God.

"Even if an unjust charge be brought against him, he will not care much.

"Nor again will he vainly exult, if through others he be justly vindicated.

"For he considereth that I am he who searcheth the reins and hearts, who judgeth not outwardly and according to human appearance.

"For often in mine eyes that is found blameworthy which in the judgment of men is thought worthy of praise." [64]

63—Luke, II, 35.
64—Thomas a Kempis adds five sentences.

CHAPTER XXXIX
*That All
Grievous
Things Are to
Be Endured for
the Sake of
Eternal Life*
"My son.

"Let not the labors which thou hast undertaken for me exhaust thee, nor let tribulations wholly cast thee down, but let my promise strengthen and comfort thee in every event.

"I am able to reward thee above all measure and aim.

"Not long shalt thou toil here, nor always be oppressed with griefs.

"Wait yet a little while, and thou shalt see a speedy end of thy suffering.

"There shall come an hour when all labor and troubles shall cease.

"Insignificant and brief is all that which passeth away.

"Do earnestly what thou dost; labor faithfully in my vineyard; I will be thy very great reward.

"Write, read, sigh, be silent; endure adversities manfully; life everlasting is worth all these conflicts, and still greater than these.

"A day shall come when there shall be eternal light, infinite brightness, steadfast peace, and secure rest.

"Then shalt thou not say, 'Who shall deliver me of this body of death?' [65] nor shalt thou say, 'Woe is me, that my sojourning is prolonged!' [66] for death shall be cast into the deep, and salvation shall be perfect; no anxiety, blessed joy, sweet and noble society.

"Oh, if thou hadst seen the eternal crowns of the saints in heaven, and with what great glory they now

65—Romans, VII, 24.
66—Psalms, CXX, 5.

rejoice, who once were esteemed by the world as contemptible and even unworthy of life, truly thou wouldst forthwith humble thyself to the earth, and rather wish to be under all than to have authority over a single one; neither wouldst thou long for this life's pleasant days, but rather rejoice to suffer affliction for God, and esteem it a great gain to be counted for nothing among men.

"Oh, if these things would please thee and move thee to the bottom of thy heart, how couldst thou dare to complain but once?

"Are not all wearisome things to be endured for the life everlasting?

"Lift up thy face therefore to heaven; behold, I and all my saints with me, who in this world had great conflicts.

"Now they rejoice, now they are comforted, now they are secure, now they have rest; and they shall remain with me evermore in the Kingdom of my Father."

CHAPTER XL [67]
Of the Longing after Eternal Life, and How Great Rewards Are Promised to Those Who Strive

"My son.

"When thou feelest that the longing after eternal salvation is flowing into thee from above, and thou desirest to depart out of the tabernacle of the body, that thou mayst be able to contemplate my glory without shadow of turning, enlarge thy heart, and receive this holy inspiration with thy whole desire.

"Give richest thanks to the Heavenly Goodness, which dealeth with thee so graciously, visiteth thee mercifully, stirreth thee up fervently, sustaineth thee

67—Thomas a Kempis inserts one chapter.

powerfully, lest through thine own weight thou sink down to earthly things.

"For thou dost not receive this through thine own thought or endeavor, but through the sole condescension of heavenly grace and divine regard, to the end that thou mayst make progress in virtue and in greater humility, and prepare thyself for future conflicts, and cleave unto me with all the affection of thy heart, and strive to serve me with fervent will.

"My son.

"Often the fire burneth, but without smoke the flame ascendeth not.

"So also the desires of many burn toward heavenly things, and yet they are not free from the temptation of carnal affection.

"Therefore it is not altogether purely for the honor of God that they pray to him so earnestly.

"Such, too, is often thy earnest longing.

"For that is not pure and perfect which is tainted with thine own self-seeking.

"Pray not for that which is delightful and pleasant to thee, but for that which is acceptable to me and bringeth me honor; for when thou judgest aright, thou must prefer and follow my appointment rather than thine own desire and anything that can be desired.

"I know thy desire, and often have heard thy groanings.

"Already thou longest to be in the glorious liberty of God's children; already dost thou delight in the everlasting home and the heavenly country full of joy; but the hour is not yet come; there remaineth another time, namely, the time of strife, the time of labor and of temptation.

"Thou desirest to be filled with the highest good, but thou canst not attain it now.[68]

"Thou must still be tried on earth, and be exercised in many things.

"Comfort shall at times be given thee, but the abundant satisfying shall not be granted.

"Be strong therefore, and be valiant both in action and in suffering things contrary to nature.

"Thy must put on a new man, and be changed into another man.

"Thou must often do what thou wouldst not; and what thou wouldst do, thou must leave undone.

"What pleaseth others shall have results; what pleaseth thee shall not succeed.

"What others say shall be heard; what thou sayest shall be accounted nothing.

"Others shall pray and receive; thou shalt pray but shalt not obtain.

"Others shall be great in the report of men, but about thee there shall nothing be said.

"To others this or that shall be committed, but thou shalt be considered of no use.

"Therefore nature will sometimes be sad, and will have to endure a severe conflict, if thou bear it with silence.

"In these and in many such instances the faithful servant of the Lord is wont to be tried, how far he can deny and break himself in all things.

"There is scarcely anything wherein thou hast such need to be mortified, as in seeing and suffering those things which are contrary to thy will; especially when that is commanded to be done which seemeth to thee inexpedient and of little use.

68—Thomas a Kempis adds one sentence.

"And because thou darest not resist a higher power, being under authority, therefore it seemeth hard to thee to walk at the nod of another, and to give up thine own opinion.

"But consider, my son, the fruit of these labors, their swift end, and the exceedingly great reward; and thou shalt not grudge to bear them, but shalt have the strongest comfort for thy patience.

"For instead of that trifling will which now thou so readily givest up, thou shalt ever have thy will in heaven.

"There shalt thou surely find all that thou mayst wish, all that thou canst desire; there it shall be within thy power to have all good, without fear of losing it.

"There shall thy will ever be one with me; it shall wish nothing out of place, nothing for itself.

"There none shall withstand thee, none shall complain of thee, none shall hinder thee, nothing shall stand in thy path; but all things desired shall be present, and satisfy thy whole affection and fill it up to the brim.

"There I will give thee glory for the scorn suffered here, a garment of honor for sorrow, for the lowest place a king's seat in all eternity.

"There shall the fruit of obedience appear, the pain of repentance shall become a joy, and the humble submission shall be gloriously crowned.

"Now therefore bow thyself humbly under the hands of all, and care not who said this or ordered that, but take special heed that whether thy superior, thy inferior, or thy equal require anything from thee or beckon thee, thou shalt take it all in good part, and with a sincere will endeavor to fulfil it.

"May one seek this, the other that; may this one glory in this, that one in that, and be praised a thousand times thousand; do thou rejoice neither in this nor in that, but in the contempt of thyself, and in the good pleasure and honor of me alone.

"This is what thou must wish, that whether by life or by death God may be ever magnified in thee." [69]

CHAPTER XLI
That a Desolate Person Ought to Commit Himself into the Hands of God

O Lord God, Holy Father, be thou blessed both now and in eternity, for as thou wilt, so is it done. [70]

Let thy servant rejoice in thee, not in himself, nor in any other; for thou alone art the true joy, thou art my hope and my crown, thou art my gladness and my honor, O Lord.

What hath thy servant, but what he hath received from thee, even without merit of his?

Thine are all things that thou hast given and that thou hast made.

"I am poor and in misery even from my youth up," [71] and my soul is sometimes sorrowful unto tears; at times also it is disquieted within itself because of impending sufferings. [72]

If thou give peace, if thou infuse holy joy, the soul of thy servant shall be full of melody, and devout in thy praise.

But if thou withdraw thyself, as thou art very often wont to do, he will not be able to run in the way of thy commandments. [73]

69—Philippians, I, 20.
70—Thomas a Kempis has a longer sentence.
71—Psalms, LXXXVIII, 15.
72—Thomas a Kempis adds one sentence.
73—Thomas a Kempis has a longer sentence.

O Father,[74] the hour is come that thy servant is to be proved, that he should be little regarded, humbled, and worn out in the eyes of men; should be wasted with sufferings and languors; to rise again with thee in the dawn of new light, and be glorified in heavenly places.

It is good for me, Lord, that thou hast humbled me, in order that I may learn thy righteousness, and cast away all haughtiness of heart and all presumption.[75]

Father, I commit myself to thee, and all that is mine for chastisement, for it is better to be punished here than in the future.

Thou knowest what is expedient for my progress, and how much affliction serveth to scour off the rust of sins.

Do with me according to thy desired good pleasure, and disdain not my sinful life, known to none so thoroughly and clearly as to thee alone.

Grant me, O Lord, to know that which I should know, to love that which I should love, to praise that which pleaseth thee most, to value that which seemeth valuable to thee, to abhor that which in thy sight is filthy.

Suffer me not to judge according to the sight of outward eyes, nor to give sentence according to the hearing of the ears of ignorant men; but to discern in true judgment between visible and spiritual things, and above all to be ever seeking after the will of thy good pleasure.

74—Thomas a Kempis has, "O Father, righteous and ever to be praised." A little further he invokes God three times more in one paragraph of three sentences.

75—Thomas a Kempis here and further below makes more addition.

How much is a man better because by man he is esteemed very great?

The deceiver deceiveth the deceitful, the vain man the vain, the blind man the blind, the sick man the sick, when he exalteth him, and in truth doth rather put him to shame, while he so vainly praiseth him.

For as the humble Francis [76] saith, "What each one is in thine eyes, so much he is, and no more."

CHAPTER XLII
That We Must Employ Ourselves in Humble Deeds, When Strength is Wanting for the Higher Virtues

"My son, thou art not always able to continue in the very fervent desire after virtues nor to persist in the higher region of contemplation; but thou must needs sometimes descend to lower things because of thine original corruption and bear the burden of this corruptible life even against thy will and with weariness.

"As long as thou carriest a mortal body thou shalt feel weariness and heaviness of heart.

"Thou oughtst therefore to groan often in the flesh because of the burden of the flesh since thou canst not devote thyself unceasingly to spiritual exercises and divine contemplation.

"Then it is expedient for thee to flee to humble and exterior works and to strengthen thyself with good actions, to expect with a firm confidence my coming and heavenly visitation, to bear patiently thy misery and the dryness of thy mind till I shall again visit thee and set thee free from all anxieties.

"For I will cause thee to forget thy painful toils,

76—St. Francis.

and to enjoy inward rest; I will spread before thee the fields of the Scriptures, that with an enlarged heart thou mayst begin to run in the way of my commandments.

"And thou shalt say, 'The sufferings of this present time are not worthy to be compared with the future glory that shall be revealed in us.' "

CHAPTER XLIII
That a Man Ought Not to Reckon Himself Worthy of Consolation but More Worthy of Chastisement

O Lord, I am not worthy of thy consolation, nor of any spiritual visitations.

And therefore thou dealest justly with me, when thou leavest me poor and without consolation.

For though I could shed tears like the sea, still I should not be worthy of thy consolation.

Therefore I am not worthy of anything but to be scourged and punished, because I have grievously and often offended thee, and in many things I have greatly sinned.

When therefore the truth is said, I am not worthy even of the least comfort.

But thou gracious and merciful God, who willest not that thy works should perish, to proclaim the riches of thy goodness to the vessels of mercy, vouchsafest even without his desert to comfort thy servant above human measure.

For thy consolations are not like human discourses.

What have I done, O Lord, that thou shouldst bestow any heavenly comfort upon me?

I do not recall having done anything good, but I

have always been prone to sin, and slow to amendment.

This is true, and I cannot deny it.

If I spoke otherwise, thou wouldst stand against me.

What have I deserved, for my sins, but hell and everlasting fire?

I confess in truth that I am worthy of all scorn and contempt.[77]

What shall I say, guilty that I am, and filled with shame?

I can speak nothing but this word, that I have sinned, Lord, I have sinned; have mercy on me, forgive me!

What dost thou so much require of a guilty and miserable sinner, as that he be contrite, and that he humble himself for his offenses?

In true contrition and humiliation of heart is born the hope of forgiveness, the troubled conscience is reconciled, lost grace is recovered, man is preserved from wrath to come, and God and the penitent soul meet together with a holy kiss.

Humble contrition for sins is an acceptable sacrifice unto thee, Lord, giving forth a savor far sweeter in thy sight than incense.

This also is that pleasant ointment which thou wouldst have poured upon thy sacred feet, for a broken and contrite heart thou hast never despised.

Here is the place of refuge from the wrathful face of the enemy; here is purged and washed away whatever defilement and pollution have elsewhere been contracted.

77—Thomas a Kempis adds one sentence and a few words.

CHAPTER XLIV
*That the Grace
of God Does
Not Join Itself
to Those Who
Relish Earthly
Things*

"My son.

"Precious is my grace; it suffereth not itself to be mingled with external things, nor with earthly consolations.

"Thou oughtst therefore to cast away all things which hinder grace, if thou desire the infusion thereof.

"Dwell gladly with thyself alone; seek conversation with none; but rather pour out devout prayer unto God, that thou mayst keep a contrite mind and a pure conscience.

"Count the whole world as nothing; prefer devotion to God before all outward things.

"For thou wilt not be able to devote thyself to me and at the same time take delight in transitory things.

"Thou oughtst to remove thyself far away from acquaintances and friends, and keep thy mind free from all temporal comfort.

"So the blessed Apostle Peter beseecheth that Christ's faithful ones keep themselves in this world as strangers and pilgrims.[78]

"Oh, how great a confidence shall there be to the dying man whom no affection to anything detaineth in the world.

"But to have a heart so separated from all things, a sickly soul doth not as yet comprehend; nor doth the carnal man know the liberty of the spiritual man.

"Nevertheless, if he would be truly spiritual, he must renounce both those who are far off and those who are near, and to beware of no man more than of himself.

78—I Peter, II, 11.

"If thou conquer thyself perfectly, thou shalt very easily subdue all things besides.

"The perfect victory is to triumph over one's self.

"For he who keepeth himself in subjection, in such manner that his sensual affections be obedient to reason, and reason in all things obeyeth me, he truly is conqueror of himself, and lord of the world.

"If thou desire to mount to this height, thou must begin manfully and lay the ax to the root, that thou mayst pluck up and destroy the hidden inordinate love of thyself, and of all private and earthly good.

"By this sin, that a man loveth himself too inordinately, almost everything is upheld which ought to be utterly overcome.

"When that evil is conquered and subdued, there will be great peace and tranquillity continually.

"But because few strive to be perfectly dead to themselves, and not fully go forth from themselves, therefore they remain entangled in themselves, and cannot be raised in spirit above themselves.

"But he who longeth to walk freely with me must mortify all his evil and inordinate affections, and must cling to no creature with selfish love."

CHAPTER XLV
*Of the Divers
Motions of
Nature and
Grace*

"My son, pay diligent heed to the motions of nature and of grace, for they move in a very contrary and subtle manner, and can hardly be distinguished except by a spiritual and inwardly enlightened man.

"All men indeed seek good, and pretend some good in their words and deeds; therefore, under the shadow of good, many are deceived.

"Nature is crafty and seduceth, ensnareth, and

deceiveth many, and ever hath itself for its object; but grace walketh in simplicity, abstaineth from all appearance of evil, sheltereth itself not under deceits, doth all things purely for God's sake, in whom also it finally resteth.

"Nature is reluctant to die and to be suppressed and conquered, to be in subjection and willingly to be subdued; grace on the other hand studieth self-mortification, resisteth sensuality, seeketh to be in subjection, longeth to be overcome, and hath no wish to enjoy freedom of its own; it gladly is kept under discipline, and desireth not to rule over any, but always to live, remain, and be under God, and is ready for God's sake humbly to bow down to every ordinance of man.

"Nature striveth for its own advantage, and considereth what profit it may reap from another; but grace considereth more, not what may be useful and convenient to self, but what may be profitable to many.

"Nature gladly receiveth honor and reverence, but grace faithfully giveth all honor and glory to God.

"Nature feareth shame and contempt; but grace rejoiceth to suffer reproach for the name of Jesus.

"Nature loveth leisure and bodily rest; grace cannot be unemployed, but gladly embraceth labor.

"Nature seeketh to possess curious and beautiful things, and abhorreth those which are cheap and coarse; but grace delighteth in simple and lowly things, and doth not refuse to be clothed with old garments.

"Nature hath regard to temporal things, rejoiceth at earthly gains, sorroweth for loss, is vexed by any little injurious word; but grace considereth eternal things, cleaveth not to temporal things, is not made sad by loss of earthly goods, and not embittered by harsh words, because it hath placed its treasure and joy in heaven, where nothing perisheth.

"Nature is covetous, doth more gladly receive than give, loveth things that are personal and private; but grace is liberal and communicative, shunneth private interest, is content with a little, and judgeth that it is more blessed to give than to receive.

"Nature inclineth to things created, to its own flesh, to vanities and vagaries; but grace draweth to God and virtues, renounceth creatures, fleeth from the world, hateth the desires of the flesh, restraineth wanderings, blusheth to be seen in public.

"Nature is glad to have some outward solace, in which the senses may have delight; but grace seeketh to be consoled in God alone and to have delight above all visible things in the highest good.

"Nature doth everything for its own gain and profit; it can do nothing as a free gift, but for every kindness it hopeth to attain either what is equal, or what is better, or praise, or favor: and it desireth that its works and gifts be valued greatly; but grace seeketh nothing temporal, and no other reward than God alone." [79]

79—Thomas a Kempis adds a long passage.

CHAPTER XLVI [80]
*That High
Matters and
God's Secret
Judgments Are
Not to Be
Investigated*

"My son.

"Beware thou dispute not of high matters, nor of secret judgments of God, why this man is so left and that man taken into such great favor; why also this one is so greatly afflicted and that one so eminently exalted.

"These things are beyond all reach of man's faculties, neither is it in the power of any reasoning or disputation to fathom the divine judgments.

"When therefore the enemy suggesteth these things to thee, or some curious people ask such questions, answer with that word of the prophet, 'Thou art just, O Lord, and true in thy judgment.' [81]

"And with this, 'The judgments of the Lord are true, and righteous altogether.' [82]

"My judgments are to be feared, not to be investigated, because they are incomprehensible to human understanding.

"Cease also from inquiring into and disputing about the merits of the saints, who is holier than another, or who was greater in the kingdom of heaven.

"Such questions often breed strife and unprofitable contentions; they also nourish pride and vainglory, [83] while one man endeavoreth to exalt one saint, and the other another; this bringeth no fruit, but rather displeaseth the saints, for I am not a God of dissension, but of peace. [84]

80—Thomas a Kempis makes this chapter follow the last chapter of the original version.
81—Psalms, CXIX, 137.
82—Psalms, XIX, 9.
83—Thomas a Kempis inserts a clause.
84—I Corinthians, XIV, 33. Thomas a Kempis adds a long passage.

"Far more acceptably in the sight of God doth he who considereth the greatness of his sins and the smallness of his virtues, and how far he is from the perfection of the saints, than he who disputeth about their greatness or littleness.

"It is more profitable to invoke the saints with devout prayers and with tears, and to beg for their glorious prayers of intercession, than to search vainly into their secrets.

"They are well, yea, very well contented, if men would but content themselves and refrain from their vain babbling.

"They glory not of their own merits, for they ascribe no goodness to themselves, but all unto me, who of my infinite love hath given them all things." [85]

CHAPTER XLVII
*That We
Ought to Deny
Ourselves and
Follow Christ*

"My son.

"So far as thou canst go out of thyself, so far shalt thou be able to enter into me.

"As to desire no external things worketh inward peace, so the forsaking of self inwardly joineth thee to God.

"I will that thou learn perfect resignation of thyself to my will, without contradiction and complaint.

"Follow me.

"I am the way, the truth, and the life.[86]

"I am the way which thou oughtst to follow, the truth which thou oughtst to believe, the life for which thou oughtst to hope.

85—Thomas a Kempis adds a long passage.
86—John, XIV, 6.

"I am the inviolable way, the infallible truth, the endless life.[87]

"If thou remain in my way, thou shalt know the truth, and the truth shall make thee free,[88] and thou shalt attain eternal life.

"If thou wilt enter into eternal life, keep the commandments.[89]

"If thou wilt know the truth, believe in me.

"If thou wilt be perfect, sell all that thou hast.[90]

"If thou wilt be my disciple, deny thyself.

"If thou wilt possess the blessed life, despise the present life.

"If thou wilt be exalted in heaven, humble thyself in the world.

"If thou wilt reign with me, bear the cross with me." [91]

CHAPTER XLVIII
That a Man Must Not Be Too Much Dejected When He Falls into Temptations

"My son.

"Patience and humility in adversities are more pleasing to me than much joy and devotion in prosperity.

"Why art thou so grieved for a little thing spoken against thee?

"Let it pass.

"It is not the first; it is not new, and it will not be the last, if thou live long.

"Thou art brave enough so long as no adversity befalleth thee.

87—Thomas a Kempis adds a few words.
88—John, VIII, 32.
89—Matthew, XIX, 17.
90—Verse 21.
91—Thomas a Kempis adds a long passage.

"Thou canst give good counsel also, and knowest how to strengthen others with words; but when suddenly any tribulation cometh to thy door, thou failest in counsel and strength.

"Consider thy great frailty, which thou dost so often experience in trifling occurrences.

"Nevertheless this happeneth for thy good.

"When these and similar trials happen to thee, put them away from thy heart, the best thou canst; and if they have touched thee, let them not cast thee down nor confuse thee.

"Bear it at least patiently, if thou canst not do it joyfully.

"Although thou be unwilling to hear it, and feelest indignation, restrain thyself; and let not any inordinate word pass out of thy mouth whereby the weak ones may be offended.

"Soon the rising storm shall be appeased, and the inward grief shall be sweetened by returning grace.

"I yet live, saith the Lord, ready to help thee, and to give thee more than wonted consolation, if thou trust in me and call devoutly upon me.

"Be more calm, and gird thyself to greater endurance.

"All is not yet lost, if thou feel thyself very often afflicted, or grievously tempted.

"Thou art a man and not God.

"Thou art flesh, not an angel.

"How couldst thou remain always in the same state of virtue, when an angel in heaven failed to do it, and the first man in paradise?

"I am he who lift up the mourners to deliverance, and those who know their weakness I advance to my divine nature."

O Lord, praised be thy word, sweeter to my mouth than honey and the honeycomb.

What should I do in such great straits and divers anxieties, if thou didst not strengthen me with thy holy discourses?

If only I may attain to the haven of salvation, what matter is it, how much or what I suffer?

Give me a good end; grant me a happy passage out of this world.

Remember me, O my God, and lead me by the right way into thy kingdom. Amen.

THE FOURTH BOOK

A Devout Exhortation
to the Holy Communion

CHAPTER I

*An Inquiry Concerning Spiritual Exercise before
Communion*

WHEN I consider thy dignity, O Lord, and mine own vileness, I tremble exceedingly, and am confounded within myself.

For if I approach not, I fly from life; and if I intrude myself unworthily, I incur thy displeasure.

What then shall I do, O my God, my Helper and Counselor in all necessities?

Teach thou me the right way; propound unto me some exercise, befitting Holy Communion.

For it is good for me to know how I ought to prepare my heart devoutly and reverently for thee, for the receiving of thy Sacrament to my soul's health, or it may be also for the celebrating of so great and divine a sacrifice.

CHAPTER II
*Of the
Examination of
Conscience and
Purpose of
Amendment*

"Above all things, the priest of God must draw nigh, with all humility of heart and suppliant reverence, with full faith and pious desire for the honor of God, to celebrate, minister, and receive this Sacrament.

"Diligently examine thy conscience, and to the utmost of thy power, with true contrition and humble confession, cleanse and purify it, so that thou mayst feel nothing weighing heavily upon thee, or know anything that bringeth thee remorse and impedeth thy free approach.

"Think with displeasure of all thy sins in general, and more particularly bewail and lament because of thy daily transgressions.

"And if thou have time, confess unto God in the secret of thy heart all the miseries of thy passions.

"Lament and be sorrowful, because thou art still so carnal and worldly.

"So unmortified from thy passions, so full of motions of concupiscence; so unwatchful over thy outward senses.

"So often entangled in many vain fancies; so much inclined to outward things, so negligent of internal.

"So prone to laughter and unbridled mirth, so hard and indisposed to tears and contrition.

"So ready to ease and indulgence of the flesh, so dull to zeal and fervor.

"So curious to hear novelties and to see beauties, so loath to embrace what is humble and despised.

"So desirous to have many things, so grudging in giving, so close in keeping.

"So inconsiderate in speech, so reluctant to keep silence.

"So disorderly in manners, so inconsiderate in actions; so eager after food, so deaf to the Word of God.

"So eager to rest, so slow to labor; so watchful after tales, so drowsy at the sacred watchings.

"So anxious to arrive at the end thereof, so wandering in attention to them; so negligent in observing the hours of prayer, so lukewarm in celebrating, so unfruitful in communicating.

"So quickly distracted, so seldom thoroughly self-collected; so suddenly moved to anger, so apt to take displeasure against others.

"So prone to judging, so severe at reproving; so joyful at prosperity, so weak in adversity.

"So often making good resolutions, and yet bringing them to so little effect.

"When thou hast confessed and bewailed these and other shortcomings, with sorrow and great displeasure at thine own infirmity, make then a firm resolution to be always amending thy life and making progress in all that is good.

"Then with full resignation and entire will offer thyself to the honor of my name, on the altar of thy heart a perpetual whole burnt-offering, even by faithfully presenting thy body and soul unto me, that thus thou mayst be accounted worthy to draw near to offer this Eucharistical Sacrifice unto God, and to receive the Sacrament of my body and blood to thy soul's health.

"For there is no oblation worthier, no satisfaction greater for the destroying of sin, than to offer one's self to God purely and wholly with the oblation of the body and blood of Christ in the Holy Communion.

"And when a man shall have done what lieth in him, and shall be truly penitent, then how often soever he shall come to me for pardon, 'As I live,' saith the Lord, 'I will not the death of a sinner, but rather that he be converted and live; because I will not remember his sins any more, but they shall all be forgiven him.' " [1]

CHAPTER III
*Of the Oblation
of Christ on the
Cross and of
Resignation
of Self*
"As I of my own will offered myself unto God the Father for thy sins, with outstretched and naked body on the cross, so that nothing remained in me that did not become altogether a sacrifice for the divine propitiation; so also oughtst thou to offer thyself willingly unto me every day in the Holy Communion, as a pure and sacred oblation, with all thy strength and affections, even to the utmost power of thy inward faculties.

"What more do I require of thee than that thou study to resign thyself altogether unto me?

"Whatsoever thou givest besides thyself is of no value to me, for I seek not thy gifts, but thee.

"As it would not suffice thee to have all things except me, so neither can it please me, whatsoever thou givest, if thou offer not thyself.

"Offer up thyself unto me, and give thyself wholly for God, and thy offering shall be acceptable.

"Behold, I offered up myself wholly unto my Father for thee; I gave also my whole body and blood for food, that I might be wholly thine, and that thou mightst remain mine.

"But if thou stand in thyself, and offer not thyself freely to my will, thy offering is not perfect, neither shall the union between us be complete.

"Therefore ought a free offering of thyself into the hands of God to go before all thy works, if thou desire to obtain liberty and grace.

1—Ezekiel, XVIII, 22-23.

"For this is the cause why so few become illuminated and made inwardly free, because they know not how to deny themselves entirely.

"My word standeth sure, 'Except a man forsake all, he cannot be my disciple.' [2]

"Thou, therefore, if thou wilt be my disciple, offer thyself to me with all thy affections."

CHAPTER IV
That We Ought to Offer Ourselves and All That Is Ours unto God, and to Pray for All

Lord, all that is in heaven and in earth is thine.[3]

I desire to offer myself up unto thee, as a free oblation, and to remain thine forever.

Lord, in the simplicity of my heart I offer myself unto thee this day to be thy servant forever, in humble submission and for a sacrifice of perpetual praise.

Receive me with this holy oblation of thy precious body, which I celebrate before thee this day in the presence of the angels invisibly attending, that it may be for the salvation of myself and of all thy people.

Lord, I lay before thee all my sins and offenses which I have committed before thee and thy holy angels, from the day when I first was able to sin even unto this hour; that thou mayst consume and burn them, one and all, with the fire of thy love; and wipe out all the stains of my sins, and cleanse my conscience from all offenses, and restore me to thy grace which I lost by sinning, fully forgiving me all, and mercifully admitting me to the kiss of peace.

What can I do in regard of my sins, but humbly

2—Luke, XIV, 33.
3—I Chronicles, XXIX, 11.

confess and bewail them, and unceasingly entreat thy propitiation?

I beseech thee, hear me and be propitious, when I stand before thee, my God.

All my sins displease me exceedingly; I will never more commit them, but I grieve for them, and will grieve as long as I live, being resolved to practise penitence, and to make restitution as far as I can.

Forgive me, O God, forgive me my sins for thy Holy Name's sake; save my soul, which thou hast redeemed with thy precious blood.

Behold, I commit myself unto thy mercy; I resign myself unto thy hands; deal with me according to thy goodness, not according to my wickedness and iniquity.

I offer also unto thee all that is good in me, though it be very small and imperfect, in order that thou mayst amend and sanctify it, that thou mayst make it pleasing and acceptable in thy sight, and ever draw it on to perfection; and bring me also, slothful and unprofitable poor creature that I am, to a happy and blessed end.

I offer also unto thee all the pious desires of the devout, the necessities of my parents, brethren, sisters, and of all those who are dear unto me,[4] and of those who have done good to me, or to others for thy love; and I commend those who have desired and besought my prayers and masses [5] for themselves and all belonging to them, whether they be living in the flesh or have passed away; [6] that all may feel

4—See introduction, p. xxviii.
5—These two words are missing in many editions.
6—This passage is missing in many editions.

the help of thy grace, the aid of thy consolation, protection from dangers, deliverance from pain; and that being rescued from all evils, they may joyfully return abundant thanksgiving unto thee.

I offer also unto thee prayers and sacramental intercessions for those especially who have in any matter hurt, grieved, or found fault with me, or who have caused me any loss or displeasure; for those also whom at any time I have vexed, troubled, burdened, and scandalized, by words or deeds, knowingly or in ignorance, that thou wouldst grant us all alike pardon for our sins and mutual offenses.

Take away from our hearts, Lord, all suspicion, indignation, anger, and contention; and whatever may hurt charity, and lessen brotherly love.

Have mercy, Lord, have mercy on those who entreat thy mercy; give grace to the needy, and make us such that we may be worthy to enjoy thy grace, and go forward to the life eternal. Amen.[7]

CHAPTER V
That the Holy Communion Is Not Lightly to Be Omitted

"Thou must often betake thee to the Fountain of grace and divine mercy, to the Fountain of goodness and all purity; that thou mayst be healed of thy sins and passions, and mayst be made stronger and more watchful against all temptations and wiles of the devil.

"The enemy, knowing what profit and exceedingly great remedy lieth in the Holy Communion, endeavoreth, as far as he can, to draw back and hinder the faithful and devout.

"For when some prepare themselves for Holy

7—This is the only place in the whole fourth book where the word "Amen" occurs, showing that here ends one original treatise.

Communion, they suffer from the insinuations of Satan worse than before.

"That wicked spirit himself, as is written in Job, cometh among the sons of God that he may trouble them by his accustomed malice, or make them too timid and perplexed, that so he may diminish their affections, or by direct assaults take away their faith, if possible to prevail upon them either to give up Holy Communion altogether, or attend with luke-warm hearts.

"But his wiles and delusions must not be heeded, however wicked and hideous they may be, but all his delusions are to be turned back upon his own head.

"The wretch must be despised and laughed to scorn, neither must Holy Communion be omitted on account of his assaults and the inward troubles he stirreth up.

"Often also too great solicitude or some anxiety or other about confession hindereth from obtaining devotion.

"Follow thou therein the counsel of the wise, and lay aside anxiety and scruple, for it hindereth the grace of God and destroyeth devotion of mind.

"Do not neglect Holy Communion because of some little vexation or trouble, but rather proceed at once to confess thy sins, and forgive freely all offenses committed against thee.

"If thou hast offended any man, humbly beg for pardon, and God will readily forgive thee.

"What availeth it to delay long the confession of thy sins, or to defer Holy Communion?

"Cleanse thyself at once; spit out the poison with

all speed, hasten to apply the remedy, and thou shalt feel better than if thou long defer it.

"If thou defer it to-day for one cause, perhaps to-morrow some greater obstacle will come, and so thou mayst be hindered a long time from Communion and grow more and more unfit.

"As soon as thou canst, shake off from thyself thy present heaviness and sloth, for it is of no use to be long anxious, to go long on thy way with a disturbed heart, and because of daily obstacles to sever thyself from divine things.

"Yea, it is exceedingly hurtful to defer the Communion long, for it usually brings on a heavy spiritual drowsiness.

"Alas, some persons, lukewarm and undisciplined, do willingly find excuses for delaying confession, and desire to defer Holy Communion, lest they should be required to keep a stricter watch over themselves.

"Alas, how little love, what flagging devotion, have they who so lightly put off the Holy Communion!

"How happy is he and how acceptable to God who so ordereth his life, and in such purity guardeth his conscience, that he is prepared and well disposed to communicate every day, if it were in his power, and might be done without the notice of others.

"If a man sometimes abstain out of humility, or by reason of some sound cause, he is to be commended for his reverence.

"But if drowsiness have taken hold of him, he must stir himself up, and do what lieth in him, and the Lord will assist his desire for the good will that he hath, which God especially approveth.

"But when any lawful hindrance doth happen, he will nevertheless always have a good will and a pious intention to communicate, and so he shall not lose the fruit of the Sacrament.

"For any devout man is able every day and every hour to draw near to Christ in spiritual communication to his soul's health and without hindrance; and yet in certain days, and at the appointed time, he ought to receive the Body and Blood of his Redeemer, with affectionate reverence, and rather to seek the honor and glory of God than his own comfort.

"For he communicateth mystically and is invisibly refreshed, as often as he devoutly calleth to mind the mystery of Christ's incarnation and passion, and is inflamed with the love of him.

"He who prepareth himself only when a festival draweth near, or when custom compelleth, shall too often be unprepared.

"Blessed is he who offereth himself to the Lord, as a whole burnt-offering, as often as he celebrateth or communicateth.

"Be not too slow nor too hurried in celebrating, but preserve the good custom of those with whom thou livest.

"Thou oughtst not to cause weariness and annoyance to others, but to observe the received custom, according to the institution of the elders; and to minister to the profit of others rather than to thine own devotion and feeling."

CHAPTER VI
*That He Who
Is about to
Communicate
with Christ
Ought to Pre-
pare Himself
with Great
Diligence*

"I am the lover of purity and the giver of sanctity.

"I seek a pure heart, and there is the place of my rest.

"Prepare for me a large upper room furnished, and I will keep the passover at thy house with my disciples.[8]

"If thou wilt that I come unto thee and remain with thee, purge out the old leaven,[9] and make clean the habitation of thy heart.

"Shut out the whole world and all the throng of sins; sit as a sparrow alone upon the housetop,[10] and think upon thy transgressions in the bitterness of thy soul.

"For every one that loveth prepareth the best and fairest place for his beloved; for herein is known the affection of him who entertaineth his beloved.

"Know thou notwithstanding that thou canst not make sufficient preparation out of the merit of any action of thine, even though thou shouldst prepare thyself for a whole year, and have nothing else in thy mind.

"But out of my tenderness and grace alone art thou permitted to approach my table, as if a beggar were invited to a rich man's table, and had no other recompense to offer than to humble himself and to give him thanks.

"Do what lieth in thee, and do it diligently; not of custom, not of necessity, but with fear, reverence, and affection receive the Body and Blood of thy

8—Mark, XIV, 14-15.
9—I Corinthians, V, 7.
10—Psalms, CII, 7.

beloved Lord God, when he vouchsafeth to come unto thee.

"I am he who hath called thee; I have commanded it to be done; I will supply what is lacking in thee; come and receive me.

"When I bestow the grace of devotion, give thanks to thy God; it is not because thou art worthy, but because I have had mercy on thee.

"If thou hast not devotion, but rather feelest thyself dry, be instant in prayer, cease not to groan and knock; cease not until thou art meet to receive some crumb or drop of saving grace.

"Thou hast need of me; I have no need of thee.

"Nor dost thou come to sanctify me, but I come to sanctify thee and make thee better.

"Thou comest that thou mayst be sanctified by me and united unto me; that thou mayst receive new grace, and be stirred up anew to amendment of life.

"See that thou neglect not this grace, but prepare thy heart with all diligence, and receive thy beloved unto thee.

"Thou oughtst, however, not only to prepare thyself for devotion before Communion, but also to keep thyself with all diligence therein after thou hast received the Sacrament.

"Nor is less watchfulness needed afterward than devout preparation beforehand.

"For good watchfulness afterward becometh in turn the best preparation for the obtaining of more grace.

"For hereby is a man made entirely indisposed, if he immediately giveth himself too much to outward consolations.

"Beware of much talk, remain in some secret place, and commune with God.

"For thou hast him whom the whole world cannot take from thee.

"I am he to whom thou oughtst wholly to give thyself, so that now thou mayst live no longer in thyself, but in me, free from all anxiety."

CHAPTER VII
That the Grace of Devotion Is Acquired by Humility and Self-Denial

"Thou oughtst to seek earnestly the grace of devotion, to ask for it fervently, to wait for it with patience and confidence, to receive it gratefully, to keep it humbly, to work with it diligently, and to commit the time and manner of heavenly visitation to God until it come.

"Thou oughtst especially to humble thyself when thou feelest inwardly little or no devotion, yet not to be too much cast down, nor to grieve inordinately.

"God often giveth in one short moment what he hath for a long time denied.

"He sometimes giveth in the end what at the beginning of prayer he deferred to give.

"If grace were always given immediately, and were at hand at the wish, weak man could not well bear it.

"Therefore the grace of devotion is to be waited for, with good hope and humble patience.

"Nevertheless impute it to thyself, and to thine own sins, when this grace is not given thee, or when it is secretly taken away.

"It is sometimes a small thing that hindereth and hideth grace, at least if anything can be called small and not rather great which obstructeth so great a good.

"And if thou remove this, be it great or small, and perfectly overcome it, thou wilt have thy desire.

"For the moment thou givest thyself to God with thy whole heart, and seekest neither this nor that according to thy will and pleasure, but settlest thyself wholly in him, thou shalt find thyself united and at peace; for nothing can give so sweet a relish, nothing can be so delightful, as the good pleasure of the Divine Will.

"Whosoever therefore shall have lifted up his will unto God with a single heart, and shall have freed himself from all inordinate love or dislike of any created thing, he shall be the most fit for receiving grace, and meet for the gift of true devotion.

"For the Lord giveth his blessing where he findeth empty vessels.

"And the more perfectly a man forsaketh these low things, and the more by contempt of himself he dieth to himself, the more speedily doth grace come, the more plentifully doth it enter in, and the higher doth it lift up the free heart.

"Then shall he see, and flow together, and wonder, and his heart shall be enlarged within him, because the hand of the Lord is with him, and he hath put himself wholly into his hand, even for ever and ever.

"Behold, thus shall the man be blessed who seeketh God with his whole heart, and receiveth not his soul in vain.

"This man, in receiving the Holy Eucharist, obtaineth the great grace of Divine Union; because he hath not regard to his own devotion and comfort, but, above all devotion and comfort, to the glory and honor of God."

CHAPTER VIII
*That a Man
Should Not Be
a Curious
Searcher into
the Sacrament,
but a Humble
Imitator of
Christ, Submitting His Sense
of Holy Faith*

"Thou oughtst to beware of curious and unprofitable searching into this most profound Sacrament, if thou wilt not be plunged into the abyss of doubt.

"He that is a searcher of Majesty shall be overpowered by the glory thereof.

"God is able to work more than man can understand.

"A pious and humble search after truth is to be allowed, when it is always ready to be taught, and studieth to walk according to the sound opinions of the fathers.

"Blessed is the simplicity which leaveth alone the difficult ways of questionings, and followeth the plain and firm path of God's commandments.

"Many have lost devotion while they sought to search into things too deep.

"Faith is required of thee, and a sincere life; not loftiness of intellect, nor depth in the mysteries of God.

"If thou dost not understand nor comprehend the things which are beneath thee, how shalt thou comprehend those which are above thee?

"Submit thyself unto God, and humble thy sense to faith, and the light of knowledge shall be given thee, as shall be profitable and necessary unto thee.

"Some are grievously tempted concerning faith and the Sacrament, but this is not to be imputed to themselves but rather to the enemy.

"Care thou not for this, dispute not with thine own thoughts, nor give answer to doubts suggested by the devil; but trust the words of God, trust his saints and prophets, and the wicked enemy shall flee from thee.

"It is often very profitable to the servant of God to endure such things.

"For the devil tempteth not unbelievers and sinners, because he hath already secured possession of them; but in various ways he tempteth and harasseth the faithful and devout.

"Go forward therefore with simple and undoubting faith, and with supplicating reverence draw near to the Sacrament; and whatsoever thou art not able to understand, commit without anxiety unto Almighty God.

"God deceiveth thee not; he is deceived who trusteth too much in himself.

"God walketh with the simple, revealeth himself to the humble, giveth understanding to babes, openeth the sense to pure minds, and hideth grace from the curious and proud.

"Human reason is feeble and may be deceived, but true faith cannot be deceived.

"All reason and natural search ought to follow faith, not to go before it, nor to come too close to it.

"For faith and love do here especially take the highest place, and work in hidden ways, in this most holy, most supremely excellent Sacrament.

"God, who is eternal and incomprehensible and of infinite power, doth great and inscrutable things in heaven and in earth, and there is no tracing out of his marvelous works.

"If the works of God were such that they might easily be comprehended by human reason, they could not be justly called wonderful and unspeakable."

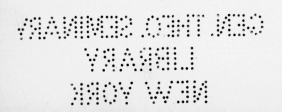